DATE DUE

THE WORLD OF TALK ON A FIJIAN ISLAND:

An Ethnography of Law and Communicative Causation

THE COMMUNICATION AND INFORMATION SCIENCE SERIES
Series Editor: BRENDA DERVIN, The Ohio State University

Subseries:
Progress in Communication Sciences: Brant R. Burleson
Interpersonal Communication: Donald J. Cegala
Organizational Communication: George Barnett
Mass Communication/Telecommunication Systems: Lee B. Becker
User-Based Communication/Information System Design: Michael S. Nilan
Cross-Cultural/Cross-National Communication and Social Change: Josep Rota
International Communication, Peace and Development: Majid Tehranian
Critical Cultural Studies in Communication: Leslie T. Good
Feminist Scholarship in Communication: Lana Rakow
Rhetorical Theory and Criticism: Stephen H. Browne
Communication Pedagogy and Practice: Gerald M. Phillips
Communication: The Human Context: Lee Thayer

THE WORLD OF TALK ON A FIJIAN ISLAND:

An Ethnography of Law and Communicative Causation

Andrew Arno
University of Hawaii

ABLEX PUBLISHING CORPORATION
NORWOOD, NEW JERSEY

Printed in the United States of America

Library of Congress Cataloging-in-Publication Data

Arno, Andrew.
   The world of talk on a Fijian Island: An Ethnography of Law and
   Communication Causation
   / Andrew Arno.
      p.   cm.
   Includes bibliographical references and index.
   ISBN 0-89391-866-0. —ISBN 0-89391-961-6 (ppb)
      1. Ethnology—Fiji—Yanuyanu Island.   2. Communication and culture—
Fiji—Yanuyanu Island.   3. Discourse analysts—Fiji-Yanuyanu Island.   4.
Social conflict—Fiji-Yanuyanu Island.   5. Yanuyanu Island (Fiji)—Social
life and customs.   I. Title.
GN671.F5A76 1992   92-21909
305.8′0099611—dc20   CIP

Ablex Publishing Corporation
355 Chestnut Street
Norwood, New Jersey 07648

To
The Memory of Klaus-Friedrich Koch

Table of Contents

Acknowledgments

I am most indebted to the people of the Lauan island that I call "Yanuyanu" in this book. They provided not only the ethnographic data but also the ideas on which this view of conflict and communication is based. I went there with a relatively blank theoretical slate—certainly with no special interest in communication as a social process—and the results of the project can only be regarded as a collaboration between myself and my Fijian conversational counterparts. I hope that disguising the name of the island, the villages, and the names of the individual actors will mitigate any possible social harm, such as embarrassment or invasion of privacy vis-á-vis the outside, that might result from this book's publication.

In any case, I am confident that the Fijian social world I encountered on the island is far too sturdy, too rich, and too confident of its own unique value to be damaged by a book of ethnography and social theory. If noticed by any other than the children of Yanuyanu who have become students of Western social science at the university level, and if perceived as negative in any detail, I trust that this book will simply add a bit of spice to to the powerful and pleasurable conflict management discourses around village *yaqona* bowls. That will be my contribution to the activity that has been so important to the evolution of my own understanding of the basic issues of social inquiry that this book addresses.

I am also indebted to the government officials who, at a time of transition to independence when bureaucratic routines were unsettled, reviewed and approved my research and smoothed my path in the field. The University of the South Pacific provided invaluable support in terms of library resources, periodic housing during visits to Suva, students to discuss the project with as it progressed, and the advice of senior professors such as Ron Crocombe, then director of the Institute of Pacific Studies. And at a personal level, I must express my special thanks to three individuals—Ropate M. Tuitaru, Olinipa Vosa, and Jope Mocevakaca—whose help and friendship made my research in Fiji such a great pleasure. I also want to thank John Harre and G.B. Milner, who gave me some much appreciated advice about studying verbal performances.

Klaus Koch, to whom this book is dedicated, conceived and organized the comparative field study in legal anthropology of which this work is a part. More important, he was teacher, collaborator, friend, and role model to those of us who participated in the project. Just before his tragic, accidental death in Cairo in 1979, Klaus wrote a circular letter addressed to several of his former students in which he declared that after wrapping up his then current research projects in the Middle East he intended to return to the Pacific, where he would concentrate on "communication about conflict." Although he did not live to carry out that goal, I like to think that this book is in some sense a continuation of our collaborative project.

My fellow participants in the comparative study—Don Brenneis, Wynne Furth, and Tisha Hickson—were a source of perspective and encouragement in the field. Tisha and I later married, and the ideas in this book have evolved and been modified by our discussions over the years. She and our daughter Claudia are a continuing source of general inspiration as well.

Finally, I would like to thank those of my colleagues in communication and in anthropology who read early versions of the book and made helpful comments. They include Majid Tehranian, Don Brenneis, Lamont Lindstrom, L. S. Harms, Richard Vincent, and Robert Anderson.

Preface
Travelers in Discourse Analysis

The British naturalist and writer W. H. Hudson, well known in the early part of this century for many popular books about birds and the ecology of rural life, reports a conversation he had at breakfast in a commercial hotel in Bristol. Hudson noted the impeccable linen, well cut suit, and heavy gold chain of the impressive and well spoken elder salesman across the table. The man talked confidently and with persuasive eloquence about the larger issues in politics and economics.

He assumed that Hudson was also a commercial traveler—although obviously of somewhat inferior rank—and after Hudson had made some detailed comments about English agriculture the older man remarked: "I perceive that you know a great deal more about the matter than I do, and I will now tell you why you know more. You are a traveller in little things—something very small—which takes you into the villages and hamlets, where you meet and converse with small farmers, innkeepers, labourers and their wives, with other persons who live on the land...Now I am out of all that; I never go to a village nor see a farmer. I am a traveller in something very large" (1921, pp. 2–3).

Academics seem to divide the world in a similar way; some hobnob with the grand ideas, and others are more at home with small details. The result is that products circulating within the intellectual economy vary by size and take their exponents into different parts. The analysis of discourse, for example, comes in two sizes: big and little.

Travelers in the big varieties speak confidently about societal, perhaps civilizational issues. Thus Foucault traces the history of entire systems of thought in his "archaeological" explorations of such topics as madness and punishment that mark the defensive perimeters of a total system of thought and action (1965, 1977). In his later work Foucault moves from examination of the historical substance of societal discourse to the analysis of the structure of discourse and the mechanisms with which it attempts to perpetuate itself (1972, 1981).

In contrast, the tradition of concentrating on the small object of analysis in discourse studies is predominant in Anglo-American social inquiry.[1] In a recent critical review of the more influential lines of thought in this area of discourse analysis, Hymes (1986) chooses to examine work in sociolinguistics, pragmatics, conversation analysis, and the ethnography of speaking. Each of these areas focuses on the details of everyday language use, and each derives from a different disciplinary approach, with correspondingly differing emphases in theory, method, and goals. All of them, however, take a somewhat similar view of what discourse is, and current models in linguistics portray it as a level or stratum of analysis. Coupland (1988), although citing ongoing debate about the details, describes the widely accepted Hallidayan framework as dividing language into three levels: phonological, lexico-grammar, and discourse. An opposition remains, however, between this linguistic conception of discourse and that implied in analyses of the large-scale discoursive formations that define societies.

The pattern here is familiar. In many areas of academic analysis, including economics, political science, and sociology, micro and macro traditions flourish side by side, and the question arises in each case as to how the two can be articulated. While an appealing answer may be that the two are simply complementary, representing analytical preoccupations with different aspects of a single object, Giddens (1979) argues that this stance cannot be maintained and that the two approaches characteristically derive from quite different basic assumptions.

This book, focusing on the ethnography of conflict management, is concerned with the problem of linking the small with the large in discourse analysis. I would locate my own approach at an intersection of the ethnography of law, which I will discuss in the first chapter, and the tradition of the ethnography of communication, which is open at

---

[1] An exception to this predominance is the British cultural studies school, inspired by Raymond Williams and more recently led by Stuart Hall, which looks at discourse hegemony from a Gramscian perspective that emphasizes large-scale patterns of power distribution.

one end of the micro/macro scale to conversation analysis (Bilmes, 1986; Moerman, 1988) but shades into larger questions of sociocultural function at the other (Brenneis & Meyers, 1984; Watson-Gegeo & White, 1990).

But elastic boundaries do not mean that the conceptual integration of micro and macro analyses has been achieved. A fundamental lack of clarity is apparent when one attempts to make use of the ethnography of speaking or communication in the specific subarea of conflict management and law.

In the project reported upon in this book, the objects of description are ordering processes. My argument is that several kinds of order are involved, and they have to be recognized analytically before one can understand how they interact. One is not confronted with a single seamless process of social ordering that can be approached from either macro or micro perspectives.

Rather, I think, there are three kinds of order that are woven together in social action: linguistic order, social order, and physical order. The weaving together is accomplished by two systems of control and creativity: a language system and a communication system. From the perspective I adopt, what I have called the small trend in discourse analysis starts from a concentration on the language system, viewed from different disciplinary vantage points, while work in the big tradition has characteristically started from examination of the communication system.

Clearly, the two traditions are interlinked in their concern for social relationships. Sociolinguistics, although taking the linguistic perspective, has characteristically concentrated on the distribution of languages, dialects, or styles of language within a community. Bernstein (1971), for example, studied the differences between middle-class and working-class ways of talking and related the two codes, "elaborated" and "restricted" respectively, to ways of life and to social mobility. From a different point of view, Labov (1973) showed how varieties of language in the American inner cities could vary without losing effectiveness in their specific situations of use.

Pragmatics, on the other hand, originates primarily in philosophy, and one of its prominent accomplishments has been the identification and analysis of the kinds of speech acts, such as commands, promises, and so on that characterize not only relations between language and the world but also between speaker and hearer (Austin, 1965; Searle, 1976). The rules that govern conversation have also proved a fruitful area of philosophical investigation (Grice, 1975), examining the ways that speech acts can fit together to constitute social action. Bilmes (1986), for example, makes use of this kind of approach in investigating the ways people can and cannot talk "reasonably" about positions they have taken in decision-making contexts.

Conversation analysis, a rebel branch of sociology in the same sense that the two sources of discourse analysis just mentioned represent minor rebellions against the mainstream in linguistics and philosophy, also looks for rules governing natural conversational sequences (Moerman, 1988; Sacks, Schegloff, & Jefferson, 1974, Schegloff, Jefferson, & Sacks, 1977); such work has shown the precision with which rules that conversationalists are completely unaware of—as long as the rules are obeyed—control turn taking, topic changing, and other universal features of everyday talk.

The ethnography of speaking derives from anthropology, and Hymes (1986), who is a seminal figure in its development, asserts its traditional anthropological role as a brake on facile overgeneralization in Western social inquiry. Bernstein's codes, for example, as well as Austin's speech act types and Gricean conversational postulates have been applied to the analysis of talk in cultural contexts far removed from those in which they were originally derived. Hymes argues that such conceptualizations can usefully serve in identifying dimensions that should be looked at in various contexts, but they cannot be expected to represent categories into which all forms of talk can be fitted. Asserting a kind of ethnographic imperative, Hymes shows that each cultural setting demands discourse analysis based on direct, specific observation that is open to the nuances of the case.

Hymes's concern with the process of generalization in discourse analysis points up the global intent of these small-scale analyses. In general, they do not see themselves as restricted to explaining micro events but as dealing with major issues in micro settings. To paraphrase Homans, minutiae is not *what* they study, but *where* they study. Still, micro analysis of communication events always invites criticism from those who see it as unable to deal with, if not an evasion of, crucial social issues such as the distribution of wealth and power along lines of class, gender, race, or empire.

In my own view of the problem, I depend upon the Saussurean distinction between language and speech but, like the exponents of the ethnography of speaking, assume that communication also has an explorable structure and that it operates as a system. The integration of the two, language and communication, becomes especially apparent in a study like that of Ochs (1988), in which acquisition of both language and culture is traced in detail. They are not parallel but interdependent. In real life the two are never encountered apart, and it is difficult to think of them separately.

And yet, they are not the same thing. Virtually any detail of language can be used to serve a critical communication function in society, but it is not rigidly linked to any such function. In a Fijian village, like the one I describe in this book, language may indicate respect or deference between people. A exploration of the language would reveal layer after layer of features that might serve to express the relationship. For example, at the level of style, the choice of words could be critical. In the Lau Group, where I worked, a well defined "chiefly language" was used historically—and still can be used at certain times—to refer to and address high nobles. In that form of language, an elaborate system of metaphors governs reference to parts of a chief's body, for example.

At another level of analysis—the semantic—certain kinds of things can or cannot be referred to if respect is to be indicated. Sexual references might be avoided between brother and sister, for example. Speech act analysis would also be appropriate because variation in the manifest intent of the utterance can also indicate respect or lack of respect; a higher-ranking person may address a command to a social inferior, but respect and deference would not permit a command in the other direction.

Other features of language, at the level of pragmatics, could also be seen to come into play. Tempo and pitch help to define the deliberate, dignified expression characteristic of *vakaturaga* speech (Arno, 1990), such as would be appropriate in addressing high nobles.

In order to understand the social reality of deference and hierarchy in a Fijian village, then, one can delve more and more deeply into the details of language. And yet language alone does not entirely encompass the phenomenon of the social relationship of respect. Virtually every other kind of behavior can also be used to signify—or perhaps more accurately to embody—the object in question. For example, one's posture, clothing, position of seating, and endless other details—which could never be exhaustively cataloged because they are continually created afresh in the specific situation—are used by Fijians to establish and express the fact of social hierarchy.

The relationship—in this example, respect—in a profound sense *is* a pattern of message exchange. It is a communication pattern, and it is constituted by an array of social codes that go far beyond language. Further, the relationship of respect is only one of a number recognized in the particular community, and each has meaning only in reference to the others. The totality of these relationships, constituted as communication patterns and capable of combining with one another to form higher-order patterns of social practice in the group, is what I call the communication system.

In action, the communication system of a group is its social life. As a body of expectations based on previous experiences of social practice, it is the group's social structure. To put it another way, the language system of the group is a set of signs and rules for their combination; in use the language system produces sentences. The communication system, by contrast, is a set of recognized social relationships together with rules that govern patterns of communication—through language and through every other medium of message exchange—among the social entities that bear those relationships to one another; in use, the communication system produces social institutions and routine practices that constitute economics, politics, and other social processes that link members of a community to one another and to their environment.

The language system of a group, as Saussure pointed out, has its own existence apart from the social use to which it is put. The same language might be used by people in countries with quite different economic, political, and artistic institutions. Natives in England, America, and India may carry out daily chores and social interactions using English, and no doubt at times they use the same words quite differently in terms, for example, of referents and implied relations among participants in the speech event; from a Wittgenstinian, use-based semantic perspective, one might argue that the various language games involved do not possess a core of common attributes that can be said to define a language. Wittgenstein (1967, p. 32e) contends that there isn't any language apart from use, and the various language games people engage in are only linked by a "family resemblance" consisting of a set of interlocking but not cross-cutting similarities in various features.[2] Even if only in this weak sense, however, people involved in sharply distinct contexts of use are drawing upon a partly shared body of phonetic, syntactic, and semantic rules. The common features, therefore, if not thoroughly uniform across cases, are at least

---

[2] In *The Blue and Brown Books* (1954, p. 81), Wittgenstein says: "We are not...regarding the language games which we describe as incomplete parts of a language, but as language complete in themselves, as complete systems of human communication." The kinds of games referred to might include such things as how to talk about color and also the technical words and usages pertaining to some trade or academic field. The popularly accepted view would seem to agree with Saussure's conceptualization, however, in which all the possible "games" of a specific speech community somehow add up to a total language that no one individual can fully command but which can be thought of as existing at the group level. One could follow this logic further and argue that different languages such as English, Fijian, German, and so on are games that add up to an entity called language in general that exist at the collective level of the human species. Here again, no one person is initiated into them all, but any person could learn any one of them. In his later work Wittgenstein forcefully rejects this notion, and his

not totally defined by specific application. This sense defines the degree to which a language can be said to be independent of the use to which it is put.

With the communication system, however, no such isolation is possible. The communication system encompasses rules that govern relationships among people, including relationships of power. Access to, distribution of, and use of material resources are also governed by rules that enforce patterns of communication within the group. Material objects are part of the process in that they are tied to meanings, and in their patterns of circulation, even without words, they constitute messages that confirm or create social relationships. Food, for example, in being given or taken, produced and used in some relation to the claims of others, is a message about relations between and among groups and individuals.

Beneveniste (1971) argues against the separation of language and discourse, citing the fact that certain words like "I," "you," and "here," and "there," and so on, are undeniably part of language but have meaning only in speech situations. But as part of the language system they refer only to an ideal speech situation that is as universal and empty of specific empirical content as the human experience of the subjective and the objective. When they are spoken, "I" and "you" are fleshed out by the social identities and relationships involved, and they are engaged in creating or maintaining a communication system.

This book is intended as a theoretical exploration of the concept of the communication system as a tool of social inquiry, and it is also intended as an ethnographic exploration of conflict management on a Fijian island. Conflict management, as a social process, will be seen as a "statement" or "utterance" framed in terms of the specific communication system of the Fijian community I studied. In this sense, I talk about conflict discourse in the big tradition. But at the same time I look at the role of language in conflict management, following in the small tradition of discourse analysis. The integration of the two is the task of theoretical elaboration.

The plan of the book is as follows. The first chapter is a subjective account of the circumstances of my fieldwork in Fiji; in it I trace the development of the theoretical stance I have adopted and discuss the

---

use-centered point of view is very fruitful in thinking about "systems of human communication." But Wittgenstein's assertion that there is no language system that is abstracted from communication events seems difficult to accept. In Chapter 6 I argue that Wittgenstein's earlier view of language, set out in his *Tractatus* and which is consistent with Sausurean linguistics, is not incompatible with his later arguments about communication systems in which language plays a prominent part.

relationship between myself as ethnographer and the community studied. With the perspective of hindsight, I try to look at the relationship from both sides. The reader is invited to interpret the facts presented and the judgments offered throughout the book in light of the situation that produced them.

Chapter 2 makes a theoretical argument that supports the idea of the communication system as an analytical device and as an object of ethnographic description. Three worlds are postulated: the inner world of the individual imagination, the outer world of physical reality, and the social world of human community operating in a culturally construed physical environment. Social science is confronted with a complex interweaving of these three worlds in the reality of social life, and its success depends on developing an appropriate model of causation. In Chapter 2, I argue that communicative causation, which is an account of cause and effect in social situations, can be understood in terms of an interaction among the regimes of causation that pertain to the three worlds. Before advancing to a more specific theoretical discussion of the connection between conflict talk and communicative causation, I accept the Hymesian ethnographic imperative, describing in Chapters 3, 4, and 5 the particular communication system in place on the Fijian island I studied.

Chapter 3 is an examination of the castelike hierarchical relationships among groups on the island. This pattern is exemplified at the level of patrilineal, landholding subclans, *mataqali*, by the division between the "nobles," *turaga*, and the "land people," *vanua*. Ceremonial exchanges among groups on the island are guided by the framework of rules for communication that constitute the communication system. The flow of messages—embodied not only in presentations of words but also in those of dance, food, and valuables—establish, confirm, or negotiate the structure of the communication system itself at the same time that they constitute the economics, politics, aesthetics, and other institutions of the community.

Chapter 4 continues the analysis on another level, describing the individual-centered regime of kinship on the island. The relationship system, based on kinship and governing all aspects of island life, is described in terms of the rules of communication that govern how participants in the system interact. The patterns of authority, joking, and avoidance thus created are then related to the political economy of the island.

In Chapter 5, a specific function of the communication system, that of conflict management, is described as a linking together of relationship system roles and defined speech events that bear upon conflict, such as joking, debate, discussion, and criticism. Specifically, I analyze the communication networks represented by informal kava drinking patterns as they bear on conflict management in the village.

Chapters 3, 4, and 5 can be looked at as an exposition of the small objects of analysis in exploring conflict management in the village. As an account of the rules of talk and the recognized kinds of talk in the community, this part of the analysis is consistent with the goals and findings of the ethnography of speaking. In Chapter 6, however, I go on to link the everyday, small-scale activity of talk and the flow of objects and performances in the village to the larger concern of the governing regime of communicative causation.

Drawing on the insights of philosophers of meaning like Peirce and Wittgenstein, I maintain that the discourse of conflict management in the specific group reflects the operation of communicative causation. The process described involves interlinked moments of shifting polarity between language and world: picturing and constructing, reliance and compulsion. From this perspective, the communication system and the regime of communicative causation it generates in the group are seen as both the medium and the product of conflict management.

In Chapter 7, using the recent military coups in Fiji as an example, I develop the notion of control communication (Arno, 1985a), examining the range of conflict management institutions, each representing a complementary or competing regime of communicative causation, that are brought to bear in situations of societal conflict. Societal conflicts, I argue, are those that engage the operation of all such institutions, exposing the patterns of their interrelationships. In Fiji, the military takeover of the government represents a societal conflict, and the ways of talking about, justifying, attacking, understanding, and acting in regard to the coups at the level of village discourse include kinship, the chiefly system, the church, and modernism. At the national and regional levels other competing communication systems and their associated/constituting institutions of conflict management seek to come into play.

This book, then, represents an attempt to deal in an integrated fashion with the "big and the "little" of discourse. Focusing on the discourse of conflict management, I explore the linkage between everyday communication about conflict, through talk and other forms of message exchange among individuals and groups, and large-scale societal conflicts and the institutions that shape societal change through the entrenchment of cominant forms of communicative causation. The book also represents a dombination of ethnography and theory, developing a theory of the relationship between conflict and communication that demands ethnography as a theoretical necessity.

Chiefly House on Yanuyanu

1

The World is Talk: Problem, Setting, and Personal Perspective

E veitalanoa ga na vuravura. Kevaka ko kila a vosa, e sega sara na ka ko na ta' rawata kina.

The world is just talk. If you know how to talk, there is nothing at all you cannot get with it.

Tui, a citizen of Yanuyanu

WADING ASHORE

Early in July 1970, I waded ashore for the first time at a small island in the Southern Lau Group of Fiji. It was an overcast, rainy evening, and I was grateful to be there finally. I had spent a week on board the cargo boat *Uluilakeba* as it hopped from one island to the next, pausing here and there to wait for a tide or to shelter from bad weather. The seas had been rough, and I had been seasick the whole time. I looked forward to an extended stay on solid ground.

As a graduate student in anthropology and part of a joint research project that linked professors and students at the University of the South Pacific and Harvard,[1] I had begun an introduction to Fijian

---

[1] The Comparative Law Project, directed by Klaus-Friedrich Koch, was funded by NIMH grant number 19531. Ron Crocombe, of the University of the South Pacific, was

language and culture in Suva, the capital city of Fiji, while I waited for the boat to sail. A government official in charge of Southern Lau, still at that point a colonial district officer, had sent a radio message ahead to announce my coming to the villagers and to request their cooperation in my work.

Mixed with the anxiety of not knowing exactly what to expect on the island, I felt a certain confidence that at least my research problem, although very generally formulated at that point, was clear cut and important. My objective was to find out how the inhabitants of this island, remote as it was from centers of government and with only intermittent and attenuated access to police and courts, handled the conflicts and disturbances of public order that arose in their community.

What, after all, could go radically wrong with such a project? The idea that there might not *be* any conflict was not worth considering, I felt sure. Where in human experience can one find an example of perfect group consensus over any period of time? If conflict proved to be rampant on the island during my stay, I would obtain plenty of good data. On the other hand, if things ran smoothly most of the time, that would indicate the presence of a very effective, intact system of conflict management, and such a system would be well worth investigating and describing. In either case perhaps something of a general nature could be learned about social conflict and its management when this particular case study was looked at in light of existing knowledge.

At the time, it was already clear that anthropological accounts of exotic conflict management institutions, such as Gibbs's (1963) description and analysis of the Kpelle moot, could have an important influence in the ongoing debate about the development of alternative dispute resolution mechanisms in the United States. Many scholars and practitioners felt that existing legal arrangements in the United States were not functioning properly, and basic questions were being asked about the types of social interests involved in disputing and how those interests might be served institutionally (see Danzig, 1973 and Merry, 1982). This academic and political context provided a clear challenge for ethnography.

Access to the information I needed, of course, was a major problem. People tend not to be completely open with outsiders in matters of internal conflict. But I was not looking for anything secret or closely

field director of the project. Several parallel field studies were supported by this grant (see Brenneis, 1973; Arno, 1974; Hickson, 1975). My initial trip to Fiji was funded by a Harvard Department of Anthropology field study grant.

guarded. What I wanted to know about particular conflicts was the sort of thing that any member of the community would be expected to know. Rather than private, psychological, personal dimensions of social conflict, I proposed to study the public aspects. My frame of reference for the inquiry was the anthropology of law, and what I knew about it so far led me to expect some sort of forum—specific to the relevant social unit to be sure, and perhaps different in many unantici-pated dimensions of format and style from known examples—in which conflict cases were expressed, discussed, and resolved in some degree (Nader, 1965). The Cheyenne (Llewellyn & Hoebel, 1943) had their way of doing it, and so did the Barotse (Gluckman, 1955), the Ifugao (Barton, 1919, 1938), the Tiv (Bohannon, 1957), the Kapauku (Pospisil, 1971), the Jale' (Koch, 1974), and all the others enshrined in the literature. They all had rules, and they all had ways of enforcing them. The Lauans were hardly likely to prove an exception.

The anthropology of law, as the field had evolved in the early 1970s, also provided a method for the investigation of conflict management in any social situation. The case method, which had been patterned after the discourse routines that define the Anglo-American common law tradition, was dominant (Epstein, 1967). This method of data collec-tion and presentation, although not immune even at that point from critical examination, may have borrowed authority and a sense of naturalness from the entrenched position it enjoyed in the culture of the ethnographers themselves. Certainly in my own case, as a recent law school graduate, I tended not to look much further than the case method as a flexible, universal way of grasping the essence of the particular system, however exotic.

It had been in law school, at the University of Texas in the late 1960s, that I had caught a glimpse of something that eventually led me to the island. What I saw was the tremendous influence of law on ordinary, everyday life. Behind the innumerable, seemingly natural and uncalculated details of daily life lay a highly ordered structure of rules (Hart & Sacks, 1958) of which most people were totally unaware. Knowing even the basic principles of law in property, contracts, and torts made sense of routine activities that most people engaged in them never questioned.

The discovery of unsuspected order at one level, however, quickly leads to further questions. If law makes sense of routine social practices, what makes sense of law? Is there yet another level of rules and principles that law itself, as a social practice, obeys unknowingly? At this point I encountered the sometime less than subtle defenses that academic law has thrown up around its perimeters. Conventionally enforced ignorance creates a moat supplemented by walls of disdain for the "soft," "nonrigorous" substance of the social sciences and the "irrationality" of politics and ideology (Unger, 1986). The odd thing is that these defenses are inward facing. Pursuing legal research, one is allowed to reach black letter law, or perhaps principles of decision that are agreed to lie behind it, but at that point all questions must cease. Here the practical nature of law overides the academic. Making legal questions empirical rather than strictly deductive can be harmful to the system. Such a line of questioning undermines the aura of fixity and finality that is law's chief functional asset.[2]

Accordingly, jurisprudence and comparative law, two largely untrod paths out of academic isolation, are weakly represented in law school curricula—a situation that could be quickly remedied by placing questions from these areas on the state bar exams.[3] In my own readings and courses in jurisprudence, I was intrigued by the regularity with which some of the early, classic authors made reference to the law of "primitives" or "savage society" in framing their basic assumptions about the place of law in social life (e.g., Vinogradoff, 1920; Austin, 1861; Pound, 1942; Kelsen, 1943). Knowing as little as I did about anthropology, I still felt sure that I knew more than most of these authors. And being overly literal in my reading of their works, I thought that their assertions were to be taken as statements of fact. Further, I assumed that careful investigation of primitive law, given the apparent importance placed upon it by some of the most respected thinkers in legal philosophy, would yield a decisive advance in the understanding of law.

It did not occur to me that when legal scholars of the pre-World War II, English-speaking world referred to "savage" or "primitive" institutions they might not be so much making factual observations as uncritically echoing a conceptual distinction between civilization, as represented by developments in recent Western history, and savagery,

---

[2] It seems clear that law exerts its influence as much by consensual obedience and nonreflective habit as by physical coercion (see Hart, 1961). To the extent that it remains unquestioned, setting the limits within which arguments must be framed, law is a powerful element of social hegemony, as followers of Gramsci have argued (see Hunt, 1982).

[3] A number of law schools in the United States do offer courses that link law to other social institutions, and a few are important centers of scholarship in this field. It can even be argued that there is a trend toward offering courses such as "law and literature," "law and anthropology," and "law and economics." Detractors among the faculty and students, who refer to such offerings as "law and a banana" courses, still represent the majority view, however (Rothfield, 1988).

which reigned in non-European parts.[4] This basic distinction was a 19th-century article of faith that justified, morally and scientifically (as long as one did not look too hard), the major economic and political structure of the era: Western colonialism.

As it happened, a formal phase of British colonialism was just coming to an end in Fiji as I began my fieldwork. Fiji became independent, after 96 years of British rule, in October 1970. As expected, Western political, economic, and cultural influence has continued unabated, however.

THE SEARCH FOR CASES

A central feature of the case method is the notion that conflicts can be packaged and academically processed—analyzed and compared with one another to produce broad generalizations—in the form of authoritative summary statements of the relevant facts and rules. In law, appellate judges provide such statements, and now anthropologists were writing them for the non-Western systems they dealt with. Of

---

[4] Some of the 18th-century philosophers of law may have seen primitive law from a Rousseauian perspective as something noble against which to contrast the evils of contemporary European practice. And, from the empirical stance of the Enlightenment, the law of primitives could be used in developing a scientific understanding of law upon which to develop a rational system. Adam Smith (1978), in his 1766 lectures on jurisprudence, cites both Iroquois and Hottentot law in discussing particular points, for example, and he argues that "to acquire proper notions of government it is necessary to consider the first forms of it, and observe how other forms arose out of it" (1978, p. 410). In more recent times, Pound's (1959) jurisprudence postulated five stages of law, starting with the primitive, and he was interested in the changes in law that followed the progression from a kin-based to an individual-centered society. The empirical perspective survives, without the evolutionary interpretation, in the jurisprudence of Karl Llewellyn, whose interest in primitive law was influenced by Sumner and Weber. Collaborating with the anthropologist E. A. Hoebel, Llewellyn examines Cheyenne trouble cases to better understand the basic functional aspects of legal institutions that apply in modern society as well (Llewellyn & Hoebel, 1941).

On the other hand, Hobbes' view of the natural state of war among men, largely adopted by the great English jurisprudent John Austin, can import a negative cast to primitive law—given that tribal peoples might be seen as somehow closer to that Hobbesean condition of *homo homini lupus* than "civilized" folk—that is taken up and reinforced by the 19th-century sense of progress and modernity that denigrates the non-Western and indirectly justifies colonialism. A trace of this pattern of thought is perhaps reflected in Kelsen's observation, in his *Pure Theory of Law*, that "primitive man probably did not explain natural phenomena according to the principle of causality" (1967, p. 82).

course in jurisprudence and in anthropology the very notions of fact and rule had been sharply questioned,[5] but absent the threat of immediate theoretical collapse, the case method still seemed solid, modified as it had been for anthropological use.

Perhaps the unalloyed legal version of the case method worked best, and helped establish its own local entrenchment in the subculture of legal anthropology, when the non-Western object of investigation was an elaborate legal system with judges and a well-developed jurisprudence of its own. Max Gluckman's (1955, 1965) remarkable success in studying the law of the Barotse in Africa had a major impact in the discipline. Other kinds of field situations quickly suggested a shift in focus from the law, as a body of doctrine, to the social process of disputing, however (Gulliver, 1963, 1971). This shift demanded the modification of the case method to include a much more elaborate discussion of the background and social context of the individual dispute as well as increased attention to the interconnectedness of cases in the community over time (Gulliver, 1969; Van Velsen, 1967; Yngvesson, 1978)[6].

My own plan of research reflected the stringent requirements of the case method as anthropologists practiced it. To deal with cases effectively, I would need to learn the language and as much about the people and their community as I could. Accordingly, I planned an initial stay on the island to begin to learn Fijian, meet people in the community, and become acquainted with the basic facts of social

---

[5] In jurisprudence, the American school of legal realism developed rule skepticism to a high point, arguing that the rule announced by the court in the particular case was automatically rewritten by the facts of that case. Therefore the rule does not determine or predict the case so much as it justifies whatever result the court reaches. This way of looking at the situation is quite similar to Wittgenstein's argument against the possibility of private rules of language that could govern or predict what people will say. An observer might object that a speaker had made a mistake, but the speaker could always claim to be following a rule. If the speaker were conceded to be the authority (such as a judge), she could say "I am still following the rule—it's just that it is more complex than you had realized."

In British social anthropology, Leach (e.g., 1961) questions the idea that the anthropologist should seek rules governing kinship, land tenure, and so on, that are analogous to jural postulates. He argues, like a legal realist, that the case defines the rule. The ethnographer, then, must examine the case with an open mind and see the "rule" in the practice of social activity.

[6] One might argue that today the movement in legal anthropology to explore the social embeddedness of law and conflict management has succeeded so well that it has accomplished the extinction of the subdiscipline. Demonstrating the centrality of its basic processes to questions of politics, economics, language, and social organization (e.g., Moore, 1978; Nader, 1965; O'Barr, 1981; Koch, 1974) the anthropology of law has become simply a form of general anthropology (but see Starr & Collier, 1989).

organization and economic activity. My project for that three-month period was a study of property as a social institution on the island.

I tried to explain that study—as an investigation of the kinds of objects, material and otherwise, that could be said to be owned, what ownership meant in terms of rights and duties, what social entities might be owners, and the rules of descent and transfer—to my hosts late into the evening of my first night on the island. Before that, however, within a few minutes of my arrival on the island, I had been escorted by several men through the dark village to the residence of the paramount chief.

There, one of the men acted as my spokesman and presented a small bundle of kava to the chief as my *sevusevu*. I had rehearsed for this ritual presentation, which was intended to acknowledge the authority of the chief and request his permission for my project, during my weeks of initial preparation at the University of the South Pacific. Having been impressed with the gravity and importance of the *sevusevu* in Fijian culture, I was surprised and maybe a bit disappointed with the brevity and nonchalance of this performance. Despite its exotic interest and personal importance to me, it was just a matter of everyday routine to my hosts.

Another surprise took place later in the evening in the house I was to occupy during my first and again during my second, longer visit to the island. Having discussed, with the help of a resident Rotuman school teacher, (fluent in Fijian and English) my property project, I revealed my longer-range objective of learning how people on the island managed conflict. Instead of reacting with suspicion or reserve, my host—the owner of the house I was to live in and a man who was to become my benefactor, advisor, and friend—simply answered the question. "The answer is obvious," Tui[7] said. Delighted to be able to solve my problem, he reached for a bundle of kava, called *yaqona* in Fijian, and held it up. "Yaqona is the policeman of the Fijian village," he said. "Yaqona together with the *tabua* take care of any trouble among us." The *tabua* is the polished whale's tooth used by Fijians in ritual presentations and petitions.

Although Tui was pleased with his answer, Inoke Alipate, the schoolteacher, looked skeptical as he translated. The other men pres-

---

[7] I have changed the names of most of the individuals referred in this book to protect their privacy in some measure. For the same reason I am using pseudonyms for the island itself and its villages. Anyone who needs to know the actual names for research purposes can easily figure them out. The meager veil of secrecy provided by this device is sufficient, I feel, given that nothing I report here, although centered on conflict, portrays any person or group as odious, evil, or the like. Obviously my purpose is not documenting local history but providing an account of the process of conflict management on the island.

ent were noncommittal, and of course I had no idea what Tui meant. Two and a half years later, as I left Fiji following my second research trip, I knew what he meant, and I felt that his words made a rather apt summary of what I had found out.

THE ISLAND

During the remainder of my first stay, I explored the island with Tui and other interested guides, mapping gardens, recording place names, and asking questions concerning ownership and use rights. The island, circular and roughly 2.5 miles in diameter, lies about 175 miles by sea from Suva. It is part of the eastern fringe of the Fijian islands, the Lau archipelago, and from the highpoint, site of an ancient fortified village, one can see the neighboring islands fading away into the distance. A volcanic island, elevated to 590 feet, Yanuyanu is covered with grasslands and has numerous rich garden areas. It is a land of agricultural abundance, unlike many of its neighbors, and has traditionally exported its surplus to other islands in exchange for timber, wooden bowls, and canoes.

Not among the lowest in the traditional political hierarchy of the Lau (Hocart, 1929; Thompson, 1940), Yanuyanu is nevertheless subject to the Tui Nayau, the Paramount of Lau, who resides on the island of Lakeba. The incumbent of that position, Ratu Sir Kamisese Mara, was also the Prime Minister of Fiji during the time of my fieldwork, and the people of the island not only collected and presented an annual tribute of yams to him as the Tui Nayau but also followed the national political events in which he was such a dominating figure.

Although isolated geographically, Yanuyanuans were interested in and informed about national, regional, and global affairs. News broadcasts over the national radio in Fijian were listened to with keen interest and functioned as a valued resource in the flow of conversation that constituted the major medium of entertainment on the island. On the eve of their country's emergence as an independent nation, perhaps Fijians—even those in remote villages—were interested in exploring the now salient possibilities of Fijian world identity. In any case, world news was considered highly interesting, and I was asked many questions about the U.S./Soviet rivalry, which had recently produced the sensational development of an American walking on the moon. Historical analogies between Vietnam and Malaysia, where Fijian special forces served under British command in the 1960s, were explored with as much interest as many strictly island matters. With a firm sense of their own local identity, my hosts seemed to want to see themselves in world perspective at this juncture in their own history.

TWO VILLAGES

Getting an idea of life in the village was another objective that I pursued. Although all in one place, the houses in the settlement are divided into two official villages and three distinct neighborhoods.[8] About 600 people live on the island, and everyone, including the school teachers at the district school, engages in subsistence agriculture and fishing. As civil servants, however, the school personnel draw salaries and live at the school compound about a mile from the village proper. The teachers are Fijians, with the exception of my Rotuman friend, from other islands, as is the district nurse who presides over the government dispensary. Ethnically, Yanuyanu, like the Lau Group generally, is homogeneous, with no families of European, Chinese, or Indian descent. Fijian is spoken exclusively.

To pay their school fees and head tax, as well as to buy European goods such as kerosene, cloth, and tinned foods, the families on Yanuyanu cut copra and make stenciled barkcloth, *masi*, to sell through the three government-sponsored marketing co-ops, one for each neighborhood. The co-ops each also operate, with personnel drawn on a rotating basis from its membership, a store from which supplies can be bought.

In the village, residence patterns roughly, and co-op membership exactly, coincide with membership in subclans, *mataqali*. The mataqali, which are the major units of social organization throughout Fiji, are the landholding entities on the island, and membership in them is determined by descent through males.[9] Within the mataqali the *bati ni lovo*, or *i tokatoka*, extended families, are the units of everyday economic cooperation, socialization, and intimate family life.

---

[8] For purposes of exposition, I am employing the convention of the ethnographic present for much general description.

[9] The mataqali, which I will refer to as subclans, are localized groups and are segments of a single larger group, the entire population of the island, that is also localized. The island polity is not itself a clan because members are not thought of as united by common descent, even remotely. The subclans on Yanuyanu belong to either of two larger groups, referred to as phratries by Thompson (1940), the "land" people, *ko ira na vanua*, and the "chiefs," *ko ira na turaga*. On Yanuyanu the land people were also sometimes referred to as the *vakavanua*, or simply the *vaka*. This classification is found

For the outsider, specifically for an American student of anthropology, life on Yanuyanu seemed to have a strong and very pleasant "village" character. The general, vague, Western category of a folk—as contrasted with mass—lifeway asserts itself at every aspect. The houses, with graceful Lauan style rounded ends and steeply pitched roofs, lie in jumbled knots along crooked footpaths in a pattern that resolves upon a large, green, rectangular ceremonial ground flanked by a white painted, Victorian-looking Wesleyan church and the impressive traditional chiefly house, which is named *Namilaika*.

Each of the village houses, or rather the *yavu*, the stone-faced, raised foundations upon which they are built, have names, and within the names a sort of covert, highly subjective history of life in the community is encoded. Few people know what more than a couple of the names mean—that is, the stories that the namings commemorated. It is a personal, family knowledge that is highly vulnerable to demographic vagaries. The names themselves, more public in character, can survive longer. Everyone knew the name Namilaika, for example, but no one I talked to could tell me how the chiefly house came to be called that. The name seems, in typical Lauan fashion, to have dark, possibly tragic connotations. Attached to the emblem of chiefly power, a magnificent house of impressive size, decorated with the large, glistening white cowries that signify things chiefly, the name asserts the co-presence of *leqa*, problems, trouble, and failure. The words themselves, *na mila ika*, mean "a type of illness associated with fish," I was told. "Perhaps a trouble that befell the village in the ancient times. No one knows now." Part of the story, and with it the relentlessly hierarchical logic of social relationships on the island, is indicated by the use of the word "mila" for illness. It is part of the

---

throughout Lau, and the two groups might be called the nobles and the commoners of each island, although this usage is perhaps misleading, given that the two groups are virtually alike in wealth, dress, bearing, and everyday routines. *Turanga* translates well as "noble" because, as in English, the term is used to indicate both the political elite and the highest and most culturally valued objects and actions. On the other hand, *vanua* also denotes something highly positive, even sacred, in traditional culture, not only a class of people—there is none of the pejorative sense of "common" in English. The relationship between the two categories is one of mutual respect, *veidokai*, according to Fijian custom, not one of domination.

The subclans are not exogamous per se, but generally men and women of the same generation within them are related as either actual or classificatory brother and sister and are not eligible to marry. While descent is patrilineal, and a married couple resides with the husband's group, there are exceptions in which they live with the wife's group and the children affiliate with her side. In the 1930s, Lauans argued before the government Native Lands Commission that they have traditionally recognized bilateral lines of descent more than was the case elsewhere in Fiji (see France, 1969).

chiefly language of Lau, a set of words and expressions that traditionally were used in reference to the high nobility (Hocart, 1929).
Ordinary folk "sa tauve mate," but the highest ranking people "sa
milamila."

People's names, like the names of their houses, represent a complex
tapestry of interwoven tales, and no one person knows more than a few
lines of the total text. There are common themes, however. People are
named for relatives from both male and female lines of descent, just as
Europeans often are, but Lauan names—more so than names in other
parts of Fiji—also represent a specific comment, lament, or reproach.
One often meets bright, happy children or prosperous, respected
adults named for the shipwrecks, falls, illnesses, deformity, survival,
recovery, or pitiable states of abandonment of elder relatives.

The interlinked systems of names remind one that coexisting with
the physical village of houses and people there is a village of symbols,
meanings, and stories in which ideas, values, social relationships,
alliances, and conflicts are the salient features of the landscape.
Needless to say, the people of the island live as much in the one village
as in the other. Names represent a point of articulation between the
two.

During my first visit to Yanuyanu I explored the physical environment and gradually became aware of the grosser outlines of the social
world, the latter being accessible only through the medium of language and knowledge of local history. When I left the island at the end
of my initial 3-month stay, my knowledge of Fijian was very limited
but I was encouraged by the occasional conversation or story that I felt
I understood completely.

COUNTER ETHNOGRAPHY

Just before I left for the first time one of the men of the village told a
story as we drank yaqona with a small group of others. The topic arose
when one of the men complimented me on my ability to sit cross-legged
on the floor for long periods instead of requiring a chair as some
Europeans might. "Andrew, here is something that happened here
that we think is funny," Tione said. "Whether you will agree is not
clear: An Englishman came here on Government business, and he was
wearing short pants, as Englishmen like to do. He came to explain
something to us, and he had a Fijian with him to translate what he
said. We offered him a chair, and he sat up on it while we sat on the
floor in front of him. Well, this man was not wearing proper underwear, and as he talked and moved his legs around, part of his testicle

became visible. Now, we Fijians are very careful not to show anything like that, but we didn't say anything. It is a highly embarrassing thing. After a while it happened again, but this time an old man who was sitting there shouted out, 'His mother's vagina! It looms into sight again!' Then we all burst into laughter. His Fijian translator knew what had happened, but he told the Englishman that we laughed because we were enjoying his talk so much. He was happy to hear that, and he laughed along with us."

I laughed very heartily at this story. So much so, in fact that later someone brought it up. "We wondered why you laughed so much," he said. "You really laughed excessively at that story." I said that maybe it was because I had been happy to have been able to understand the story so well. "Yes," he said, "and then also you were happy to be leaving soon to go back home."

The story itself, together with the later conversation, impressed me with the closeness of observation I myself, as an outsider, was under as I went about my own observations. Any variation in my routine would bring speculation and inquiry about my feelings. Was I unhappy, ill, homesick? One day, when a cargo boat visited the island—something that happened about once a month—a woman remarked to me, "You were very happy indeed today because the boat was coming and you could get your mail." "Oh, no, not particularly," I said. I was lying, but I couldn't help rebelling against such close attention. "No," she said, "you were happy. You never light your pipe in the mornings, before lunch, unless you are extremely happy."

At first I answered what seemed incessant questions about whether I was homesick in the negative because, for one thing, I wasn't, and also because I did not want to appear less than contented with the villagers' hospitality, for which in fact I was extremely grateful. Such conversations tended to go like this:

"You are homesick"

"No, I am not."

"Of course you are. The food is not good. It is not what you are used to eating."

"No, it's wonderful. I'm very happy."

"And then there is the lack of beds and chairs that you Europeans like..."

By varying my answers, however, which I eventually began to do out of boredom with saying the same thing every time, I discovered that my hosts were motivated partly by curiosity about the extent to which *kai palagi*, people of European descent, were subject to what they considered a peculiarly Lauan complaint, *tailasa*. "We Lauans are the same way," they would tell me, warmly, when I admitted to being homesick. "We go other places, but soon we find we can't enjoy ourselves, and we have to come home." I soon found this was a more agreeable conversational path than the other one.

Once, when I had completed a survey of households in the village with the help of two friends, it was suggested that we celebrate with a bowl of *yaqona*. Foolishly, I tried drinking full, large bowls full instead of the lesser amounts I usually took. After several rounds it all came up again, just as I made it to the door of the house.

My embarrassed apologies were graciously brushed aside with assurances, including details of specific instances, that even accomplished Fijian yaqona drinkers suffered the same reaction at times.[10] Much later, however, my host raised the matter again. "It is a strange thing," he said. "When we Fijians vomit, all sorts of food comes up. But when you Europeans vomit, it is only water." I assured him that it was only because I hadn't eaten anything recently.

This kind of talk seemed partly based on a keen interest in the specific peculiarities of the Europeans and the differences they displayed not only with Fijians but also among themselves. As Quain, who did ethnographic research on the large island of Vanua Levu in the 1930s, remarks, "even the most thoughtless among [the Fijians] has developed a taste for comparative ethnology which is rare among European nations" (1948, p. 2). I was told of differences between Australians, New Zealanders, and Englishmen, for example, and some people had observed the specific characteristics of German tourists as well. Villagers listened with interest to stories of conflict among nations in the Middle East, and between the Irish and the English in Northern Ireland, on the daily translation of the BBC world service over the radio.

The Fijians' interest in closely observing the habits and characteristics of Europeans seemed clearly related to their experience of colonialism. In discussing the disapproved practice of *veivakaisini*, flattery, a villager said that, for example, the English are extremely susceptible to flattery. "An Englishman loves to be treated as though he were a high chief," he said, and the other people present laughed in

---

[10] After leaving Yanuyanu, I conducted a shorter comparative field study in a mountain village on Vanua Levu. Discussing the relationship among cross-cousins, an informant explained the institution of the *qusiqusi ni lua*, vomit wiping rag. "Suppose you challenge your cross-cousin to drink a large bowl of yaqona, and he says 'No, I give up. If I drink that I will vomit.' Then you say 'Go ahead. If you vomit I'll give you my shirt to wipe it up with.' If he does vomit, you give him your shirt. Sometimes five or six men will strip off their shirts and give them to him when this happens. Of course, the shirts are never used to wipe up the vomit. A rag or a piece of sacking would be used for that, but he can keep the shirts."

recognition of this typical weakness for agreeable self-deception. He went on to tell several Figaroesque anecdotes about a Fijian he knew who had worked as a driver for an English businessman.

What seemed to be a major conventional distinction, made salient by my own origins, was that between the English and the Americans. A number of the older men in the village had participated in World War II in the Pacific, and their observations of the Americans provided the substance for stories that were still in demand during informal *yaqona* drinking sessions.

In light of news about the civil rights struggles in the United States, I was asked about the relationship of rivalry (*veiqati*) between black and white Americans. Here again, I think the villagers' interest in exploring that relationship was partly an indirect inquiry about my own attitudes toward them, and, more generally, the global question of relationships among European and non-European peoples. Leaving one form of association with the English, they were preparing to enter into another as a member of the commonwealth. Contemporary Fijian folklore, unsupported by anthropological evidence, even postulates an African origin of the Fijian people, and I recorded some joking references to this supposed identity. "Shake hands with your country-man," I was told on being introduced to a man on a footpath. "He is a Negro. His father is a black American."

One man told an anecdote, which sounded apocryphal, about an encounter between a Fijian and an African American soldier in Suva during World War II. The African American soldiers were very powerful fighters, he explained, and often engaged in fistfights with the European Americans. The Fijian saw an African American looking in a shop window and mistook him for a fellow Fijian. "*Sa bula vinaka!*" he said, in greeting. The American turned and looked at him menacingly. "What you say, boy?" he said, challengingly. (This line was told in English.) Startled, the Fijian blurted out his entire stock of English words. "Yes! No!" he cried, and then fled.

Although it was not explicitly stated, I think the national circumstances of the time raised the question of the possible terms of coexistence of European and non-European peoples within a single political framework. The villagers, ardent boxing fans, were well aware through their radio listening that one of the most famous, wealthiest, and most interesting men in the world, Muhammad Ali, was an African American. On the other hand, they knew that the political and economic position of Africans in America was not equal to that of the Europeans, and they wanted to know more about the problem.

I do not mean to imply that my Fijian hosts closely identified themselves politically or otherwise with African Americans. Perhaps they saw a vague analogy and were interested in the general problems of multiethnic societies, of which their own is a striking example, given that about 50 percent of Fiji's citizens are of Indian descent. Once I was asked during a yaqona drinking session to tell about "*ko ira na i taukei*" back in America. In Fijian "*i taukei*," a term that might be translated "the owners," is used to refer to the Fijian people. Reasoning that if they were the *i taukei* in Fiji I must be one in America, I began by saying that we Americans had come from all over the world. "No," someone said, "we want to know about the real *i taukei*, the *kai idia damudamu* (Red Indians)." Only then did I notice that I had been asked about "them," *ko ira*, rather than "you," *kemuni*. For my hosts, a major question in world history was what happens to an indigenous people when others move in.

At times I was asked directly about civil rights problems in the United States, but I think my ethnographers were interested as well in observing my reactions when the topic was introduced—as in telling the story about the African American soldier—in less direct ways. Certainly, for my own part, I valued natural conversation quite as much as more formal interviews in trying to understand the world of my hosts.

THE ART OF CONVERSATION

As I carried out my research, I found myself being trained in the art of Lauan conversation, in which, depending of course on the circumstances and purposes of the talk, ingenious, graceful, appropriate lines of argument or expressions of sentiment are valued over consistency or brute factuality.

After I returned to the island for my second visit, having spent the fall and spring semesters in further academic preparation at my university, my facility in Fijian increased, and I became even more aware of this dimension of my "data." One evening, after we had eaten dinner and were waiting for others to drop by, Tui proposed a topic of discussion.

"Here is something I would like for us to talk about," he said. "Which is the more important in the world, Religion or Learning (*na lotu se na vuku.*")

Unsure of how to express myself, I said, "Please, Tui, you go first. What do you think?"

"Religion," he said. "Religion concerns what is right and wrong. People can be very highly educated, but without religion they may do evil."

"Well, I don't agree with what you are saying," I responded. "There are many different religions in the world, and who is to say which one of them is correct. In the area of learning, all people can be in agreement, and it can lead to advancement."

"Oh, how true!" Tui said. "Actually I agree with you completely. I only picked religion because I thought that was what you would say."

Now I was curious about what he really thought. He did propose the topic, after all, so it must have been of some significance to him. I brought up the question again later when the mood of the conversation seemed more reflective. I told him I had been surprised at his answer because it seemed to me that he was rather interested in religion, seeing that he often brought it up. I didn't go on to say so, but his frequent comments about the church were generally negative, pointing out the hypocrisy or stupidity of various people in the church hierarchy.

"In truth," he said, "I don't know anything about education. My own education was very poor because when I was a child the teachers knew little more that we did. I am sure I could have done very well at school if the teachers had been good. But then I suspect that schooling is useless in any case. Children need to learn skills like farming and carpentry. As for religion, I don't know anything about that either. But I really do fear God [*rerevaka na kalou*]."

On many occasions I encountered what I came to think of as the "*butobuto* line." Sitting around, drinking *yaqona* in the evening or on a rainy afternoon, someone would talk about Fijian culture this way: "Before the coming of Christianity we were in darkness (*butobuto*). Now we are in an era of enlightenment (*rarama*)." There were many elaborations of this kind of talk, but the argument and metaphor were always the same.[11] I recorded one use of it as a group of men listened to

---

[11] Sahlins evidently heard similar talk during his ethnographic research on Moala Island, adjacent to Lau, in the 1950s. He concluded that no European can be fully accepted by the Fijians because "he is always something above them: in their view he has "light" (and is light) while they are in "darkness" or ignorance (and are dark)" (1962, p. 2). Sahlins comments that "this lesson of their history cannot now be undone." On Yanuyanu I came to view this commonly employed way of talking and analyzing situations as a line of argument, among several related ones, to be used as conversational purposes dictated. Certainly in some sense it reflects a lesson of colonial history in Fiji, but I think my perspective on it as a forensic resource is closer to that suggested by Sahlins's later work on history and culture (1985), and that of Kaplan (1990), in which the emphasis is on the logical autonomy and creativity of local culture as it interacts with European culture. In the concluding chapter of this book I

a fellow villager who had returned from the first South Pacific Festival of the Arts in Suva. He described with approval the elaborate precision of the Samoan dancers, and heaped scorn upon the efforts of the groups from Australia, whose dances he characterized as "pointless" and dancers as naked and "like animals." One of the men offered a theoretical explanation for the differences. "Enlightenment came from the East," he said. "Those who received it earliest have advanced (*toroicake*) the highest." This argument is used to explain the relative technological advancement of the Europeans also.

After hearing this idea advanced and earnestly explored a number of times, I declined to support it when called on to do so. "Why do you speak of darkness and light," I asked. "Aren't the traditional Fijian customs useful and good?"

I was surprised at the immediate and warm support given this alternate proposition about the relationship between Western and Fijian culture. Talk of darkness and light was quickly abandoned as speakers began to detail the evils of the European way of life in contrast with the wholesome virtues of Fijian customs of the land. Evidently on this question there were at least two lines of thought, contradictory in basic premise as they might be, worthy of enthusiastic support and elaboration as the occasion demanded.

In general, given that almost everything I learned on the island came from situations of this kind—informal conversations while walking, working, or drinking *yaqona*—a basic problem became clear to me as I progressed in my fieldwork. What is the ethnographer to make of conversations like these? Starting from a position of relatively naive empiricism, I was eager to learn about the substance of what was being said. What did they think about the relative merits of religion and secular learning? How does the Fijian think of his own culture in relation to that of the metropolitan world?

But how can one tell when the people one talks to move with such ease and apparent conviction from one position to another? After my research had been underway for a considerable time, a perspective suddenly occurred to me, one that should have been obvious from the start, that made sense of what I was doing.

---

specifically identify the discourse of modernity—implied by talk about *rarama* and *butobuto*—as an incipient conflict management and communication system specifying distinct identities, interrelationships , and rules of message exchange.

Another perspective on the problem of establishing the "true" attitudes of Fijian villagers from verbal evidence is provided by Hocart (1929, p. 68), who comments that directly opposing statements by the same informant were "characteristic both of the fluidity of Fijian institutions and the people's manner of expressing this fluidity by contradictory statements..."

TALKING AND DOING

About halfway through my second visit, I had settled into a fairly comfortable routine of data collection. I felt that I knew the cast of characters in general, and I had gotten to know several people well. Three or four were quite interested in what I was doing, and they were more than willing to discuss ideas and explain and clarify things that I saw or heard in my daily activities. With their help I had formulated a set of basic survey questions about demography, economics, and political organization and had interviewed every head of household, visiting virtually every house in the village. I had also conducted numerous more or less formal interviews on specific topics with knowledgeable people from a variety of social positions.

The far greater part of my activities in the village, however, consisted not in interviews, surveys, or mapping, but in listening to conversations that took place among my hosts. During daily, informal *yaqona* drinking sessions, men came and went, and the topics of conversation drifted from one thing to another. Sometimes I would be asked about my activities and experiences, or about life in my country. For the most part, however, people talked about subjects of current interest in the village. Later, in more private settings—eating meals, walking somewhere, or fishing, perhaps—I would ask one of my friends to corroborate my understanding or to explain what had been said and why. This sort of activity became more and more interesting as I came to have a basic knowledge of the personalities, relationships, and histories involved. At times I wondered whether—and I am sure my hosts wondered too—I was really doing research at all or just enjoying myself listening to local gossip, much as I would be doing back home.

Specifically, although I was filling up notebooks and audio tapes with what I looked at as background information, I was not getting the kind of *cases* I needed for my study of the indigenous conflict management system. This is not to say that I was not hearing a lot about conflicts in the village. Talk about conflicts of various kinds and intensities formed a large part of what I heard every day. Very often some event would happen that I felt sure would be the beginning of a good solid case. Since I had heard about it at the start and was on the spot, I felt sure that I could learn a good deal about the details of how people handled conflicts in the village. Here is an example from my field notes of October, 1971:

Epi, Tui's elderly father, joined a group of men drinking *yaqona* early in the evening. He told them that he was very upset—so upset that he had not eaten anything that day. He still did not feel hungry, and he wanted to drink *yaqona* for a while.

When he had arrived at his gardens that morning, he discovered that Vesu's cow had eaten and spoiled a lot of the crops. Although he had spent the whole day trying, he could neither catch the cow nor chase it away from his gardens.

Returning to the village, he had gone straight to Vesu's house and, being very angry, shouted from the path that Vesu had better see to his cow right away because it has spoiled his garden and he had speared it. He said he lied about spearing the cow because he thought it would make Vesu hurry. He was still worried because he didn't know if cows slept at night or if they continued to eat.

The other men were very attentive and sympathetic. They said Vesu was at fault for not keeping his cow tied properly, and one man recalled that the cow had gotten loose once before and had eaten the seed yams in Vesu's brother Rusiate's garden. Several men suggested that Epi report the matter to the police at Lakeba Island by wireless.

Epi said that he did not intend to do that, but that if Vesu would come to him with a tabua (whale's tooth) in the traditional ritual of reconciliation, *i soro*, he would forgive him. He went on to talk in general terms about the problems involved in keeping cows on the island. It was a new practice, and Epi argued that the island was too small for it. Some agreed, and some did not. Everyone felt, however, that in this case Vesu was at fault and that in the past he had proven himself to be a troublesome and uncooperative man, *tamata yalo kaukauwa*.

This would seem to be the beginning of an excellent case, and I tried to follow subsequent events closely. In fact, however, nothing happened. The incident was not reported to the police, the *i soro* ritual was not performed, and village life went on as usual. A few weeks later, in fact, when Vesu's son was being married, Epi participated fully in the ceremonies and festivities, and there seemed to be no restraint between Vesu and Epi.

Reviewing my notes, I realized that this was not at all an unusual turn of events. It seemed that although there was plenty of conflict to manage, the villagers did nothing. From my notes I could see that all they did was *talk* about conflict; very seldom did they *do* anything about it.

This, of course, as it suddenly dawned upon me, was exactly the answer to my problem. Somehow, talking about conflict was what they did about it, and the focus of my research would have to be just that.[12]

---

[12] Favret-Saada, investigating witchcraft in the Bocage, made this observation about her experience of the ethnographic process: "In the field...all I came across was language. For many months the only empirical facts I was able to record were words" (1980, p. 9). My study of conflict management on Yanuyanu took a similar course, and I

From that point I began to investigate talk more systematically. I asked people what kinds of talk there were and how the different types were distinguished. I collected examples whenever I could, and I found that my existing records of conversations were rich sources.

Further, I realized that the Fijians I had been talking to had already adopted this perspective.[13] Asked about the relationship between certain categories of kinsmen, informants would almost always formulate their answers in terms of communication: "They can say anything to one another," or "they joke with one another," or "they can't speak at all."

One evening, as a small group drank *yaqona*, Tui told about his experiences during a recent trip to Suva. He said that he had found that Master Inoke, the school teacher, was also in Suva, on his way back to Yanuyanu after having used the school break for a trip to Rotuma to see his relatives. Inoke, as it developed, was stranded. He had missed the cargo boat, and he had to get back to Yanuyanu as soon as possible for the start of the next term.

Tui told the group that he decided to help Inoke by showing him how to operate within the scheme of traditional Fijian social relations. Inoke often found himself receiving "lessons" of this type from Tui, who as a classificatory father of Inoke's wife, seemed determined to attend to his education in local customs.

Tui's idea was to get Inoke passage on a government ship that might be traveling to the Southern Lau for some official purpose. From connections among Fijian crew members, he learned that a suitable boat was ready to sail. The next step was to obtain permission from the government official, a Lauan of high chiefly rank, who had the authority to assign passenger space on the boat.

Having bought a bundle of *yaqona* at the market, Tui took Inoke to the government office. Acting out the scene for our benefit, he demonstrated how he had told Inoke to leave the talking to him as they

---

came to the similar conclusion that I was at first missing the most important dimension of what I was observing. As Favret-Saada puts it, "[n]ow, witchcraft is spoken words; but these spoken words are power, and not knowledge or information" (1980, p. 9).

[13] Turner, who conducted fieldwork in the eastern highlands of Viti Levu, also observes that Fijians are prone to communication-based explanations of social life. He makes the theoretical argument that "communication is the very basis of social life and, thus, exchange broadly conceived plays a major role in the continuous process of social construction." He then goes on to observe that while cultures differ in their recognition of this fact, "Fijian culture is one that stresses the importance of exchange and viewing exchange transactions as acts of communication (and thus performative acts in the construction of society) is not only analytically useful but also conforms to the Fijian view of the matter" (1987, p. 210).

entered the office. He showed how Inoke, innocent of all propriety, had walked into the office straight up, looking around. Tui tugged his arm and showed him that they had to creep forward, bent over, *qasi mai*, toward the official. Sitting cross-legged and clapping his hands in the ceremonial *cobo*, he presented the *yaqona* and explained Inoke's predicament and request. Then, having obtained the permission they sought, Tui had to lead Inoke from the room before he committed some gaffe.

Everyone present laughed at Tui's dramatic account, including Inoke, who admitted that it had happened that way. Tui triumphantly proclaimed himself a master of traditional customs and said that no one on Yanuyanu could beat him in modern business activities either. He said that he was not afraid to speak to anyone—excepting only Europeans, because he did not speak English. "The world is just talk," he concluded. "If a person only knows how to talk, there is nothing at all that cannot be obtained by it."

MAPPING THE WORLD OF TALK

It was this world of talk that I set myself to map out. In previous, shorter pieces I have presented ethnographic descriptions of what I have come to think of as the communication system of Yanuyanu Island (e.g., Arno 1990, 1985b, 1980, 1979a). In this book, written some 30 years after I first went to Fiji, I am attempting not only to put together those fragmentary accounts but also to explore some of the theoretical questions that the findings raise.

The notion of the communication system itself and its relation to social structure and organization raises questions of a general nature. For example, it requires exploring the nature of communicative causation, the mechanism whereby a message—a mere formulation of signs—can bring about real effects in people's lives. Even more fundamental is the problem of dealing theoretically with the relationship between language and reality.

Theoretical development in the area of communication and conflict management is necessary, given the contrasting views that are currently held. The realist view is that the generation and management of social conflict is determined by patterns of power and interests defined by economics and politics, with communication playing a transparent, facilitating part. The constructivist view, however, sees communication as determinative, shaping and creating facts, rules, interests, and power. It seems clear that there is truth on both sides, and an integrative position that allows partial determination to communication but does not ignore external realities requires a plausible account of the causal links between communication and social action.

Development of such an account has proved a theoretical stumbling block in the field of communication research because of an oversimple model of the orders of reality involved. My approach, which I discuss in the next chapter, delineates relations among the inner world of the imagination, the outer world of physical reality, and the social world of human interaction. The specific characteristics and the interrelationships among these worlds have been explored by Freud, Wittgenstein, Saussure, Pierce, Jakobson, and others, as well as by philosophers of natural science.

In the framework I present, describing the idea of the communication system in the following chapter, the language system arises from the interaction of the inner and social worlds, and it then penetrates and governs the logical workings of the inner world. Similarly, the communication system arises from the interactions of the social and the outer worlds, and it penetrates and governs the functional operation of the social world.

Developing an idea of communicative causation requires consideration of the distinct regimes of causation involved in the three worlds. As Freud observed, the inner world is characterized by the collapse of the distinction between image and object, which eliminates the resistance based on physical and time constraints. I call this primary causation in reference to Freud's primary process. Causation in the outer world, explored in the modern tradition of natural science since the Renaissance, fully acknowledges the resistance associated with time, space, and mass. In much of American, behaviorist social science this regime of physical causation has been attributed to the workings of the social world, but at great cost.

The recent crisis in social science and the search for new paradigms of research is a sign of the need for a more effective formulation of the causation at work in the social world. I will suggest that it might be called communicative causation and that its outline be sought in the work of Peirce, Saussure, and Wittgenstein.

I find it difficult to choose between theory and substantive ethnography as the declared focus of the book, and I would prefer not to make the choice. In some ways I now see the flesh and blood reality I encountered in Fiji as an elaborate extended metaphor with which to explore questions of language and conflict management. As I work through my notes and transcriptions, however, the primary nature of the ethnographic reality reasserts itself.

Earlier in this subjective introduction I mentioned the awareness, suggested by the ethnographic experience, of the coexistence of the physical village and the village of social meanings. Exploring the world of words and ideas with my Lauan hosts, with their particular delight in the pleasures and the power of talk, I realized that the possibilities in this realm are endless. There may be only one physical world, but there can be any number of language-created worlds.

The theme of multiple, overlapping, and impinging worlds seems especially pertinent in a place like Fiji as it seeks to deal with internal divergences and find a place in the larger world.

2

Word, World, and Rule:
Toward a Theory of Communicative
Causation

E ra veitalanoa. E ra qoro.
Waqa ni burotu rikata na soqo.
Uru liku na dreke e na koro

They talk. They are astonished
That a canoe from Paradise lurches into the gathering,
Lowering its mast in the village.

(Luan dance verse,
from Thompson, 1940, p. 77)

Focusing on communication about conflict raises a fundamental question: What is the role of communication in conflict management? Is it relatively transparent, largely serving to facilitate the expression of the facts and rules that are the real basis of the dispute management process? Or does communication to a substantial degree constitute the dispute itself and shape the outcome according to its own nature?

In a recent survey of the area of language and disputing, Brenneis (1988) observes that two camps can be discerned. "Many legal anthropologists assume the language of conflicts to be important but relatively transparent, while many linguists become so involved with textual details that sociopolitical contexts are taken for granted" (p. 221).

These two positions can be called realist and constructivist respectively. The realists believe that for all the talk that goes on, the outcome of the dispute—and the fact of the dispute to begin with—is determined by real, material interests and distributions of power. Language in dispute settings reveals, or perhaps as often conceals, these factors, but in either case its only real importance derives from its relationship to them. The constructivists believe to the contrary, as Brenneis concludes from his survey of the literature, that "the language of disputing does much more than reflect some putative 'real action' going on elsewhere in the sociopolitical sphere. Language is not an epiphenomenal reflex of other relations; indeed, it often creates and shapes those relations" (1988, p. 229).

One must also consider the influence upon talk, and social practice in general, of those aspects of nature that are not affected by human action. As Marx and Engels posed the problem, "once upon a time an honest fellow had the idea that men drowned in water only because they were possessed of the idea of gravity" (1947, p. 7). A basic difference in transitivity must be acknowledged. A social construct such as a property right or contractual obligation, once established by the weight of public opinion or the voice of authority and reinforced by parallel entrenchment within the many intertwined lines of discourse that constitute the intellectual life of the society, determines within broad limits the language used to represent it—that is, how it can be talked about. Ultimately, however, the direction of determination can run the other way: Changes in ways of talking about it cause changes in the construct itself.

A natural object, such as gravity, also determines, by virtue of its direct impact on human experience in the physical world, some aspects of the talk that refers to it. But changes in the way people talk about gravity does not change gravity. Things still fall to the ground. People still sink in water.

Of course the difference between the two cases is not so clear cut because the *idea* of gravity, itself a social construct, does readily change with changes in talk. Newton's formulation, for example, changed the way people thought about gravity and, as a cornerstone of the vision of the universe as a clockwork mechanism, had tremendous impact on religion, government, art, and the whole of Western thought.

All these considerations bear on the ethnographic problem at hand. In studying conflict management, how much emphasis should be placed on talk? Goldman (1983) argues that legal anthropology should go in the direction of much more detailed examination of the language of disputing. A dispute, after all, *is* talk, and the more closely we study talk the more we understand disputing. A realist might assert, however, that the details of language simply tell us less and less about the powerful determining factors that shape disputes and that are not significantly influenced by what people in the village say. National and international patterns of economics and power, such as colonialism or neocolonialism, are roughly equivalent to gravity from the perspective of the village dispute.

The crux of the ethnographic problem can be stated this way: What do the patterns of causal relationships between the talk that constitutes the disputing event and the social practices and natural realities external to that event imply for the study of conflict management? How deeply and in what direction does one go? That question requires a closer examination of the more basic, underlying problem of communicative causation.

DEATH BY COMMUNICATION: TWO CASES

In his study of conflict and dispute among the Jale' people of the highlands of West Irian, Klaus-Friedrich Koch (1974) recorded a rich variety of cases, some starting from seemingly trivial breaches of expectation and eventually escalating into full scale wars. This pattern owed, Koch argued, in part to the absence of overarching institutions of social control beyond the level of autonomous local wards, each of which centered about its sacred men's house.

One case that Koch observed (personal communication, 1972) concerned the Jale' men's distinctive costume, which is made of many yards of ratan coiled in hoops around the midsection—neighboring people call them the 'hooped Jale'." The material for their suits is not available in their own territory, and to obtain it men must make a dangerous trek through the mountains. In this particular case, one of the men decided that he needed a new suit and he successfully traversed the treacherous path to the source of the ratan. When he returned, his new costume was admired by everyone. It made a particular impression on one young man, who decided that he must have one too and set off to get it. He fell from a cliff and was killed during his journey.

For the Jale', this situation raised serious questions of liability for the death. According to the second man's group, his death had been caused by the actions of the first. The latter's going for new clothes had caused the youth to go, and his death was the result.

In the fall of 1986, articles in the *New England Journal of Medicine* (Phillips & Carstensen, 1986; Gould & Shaffer, 1986) reported the results of research on the relationship between suicide and media content. It was asserted that when suicides are depicted or reported in the mass media, there is a significant increase in suicides among the public. Further quantitative studies have failed to support the purported relationship (Phillips & Paight, 1987; Davidson et al., 1989), but dramatic, if anecdotal, confirmation of the hypothesis appeared few months after the initial publications. A suicide pact among four teenagers in New Jersey was widely reported on network television and in the newspapers (Hanley, 1987), and similar suicides, using the same methods and with evidence of media linkage, quickly followed in other parts of the country (*New York Times*, 1987a, 1987b.)

Both of these cases, the one from New Guinea and the other from the United States, can be interpreted as raising the issue of communicative causation. One man caused another to die by inflaming his desire for new clothes, and television content causes people to commit suicide. In both cases there was no direct physical causation. The Jale' villager did not push his victim off the cliff, and no one involved in TV programming physically assisted the suicides. In each case the instrument of death was a message—death by communication.

The Jale' case is of interest in part because it reveals a distinctive theory of liability and causation among a non-Western people. But it is also interesting in terms of the reaction it evokes among Westerners. Recasting it in American terms of reference, it seems farfetched because the chain of causation has been stretched so far. For the individualistic Westerner the intent of the wrongdoer is important, and here the culprit had—as far as we can imagine—no credible intent to harm the victim. If the first man sent a harmful message, it was an unintended message. In a common-sense sort of way, one can agree that the message did have an effect. But when it comes to blame, Westerners see the victim himself as responsible for his reading of the message and for his response to it. He yielded to his own internal impulse of vanity or rivalry, and he was himself the cause of his going on the fatal journey.

The TV case is much closer to the usual problem presented to communication research, but the same sort of issues are present. At first encounter, it might not seem to raise questions of liability. One could hardly blame the television industry, given that no one knew that the effect would be produced. On the other hand, once the correlation has been established—or at least suggested—blame and perhaps liability enter the picture with respect to future programming. The deadly effect is still unintended, but it is now not entirely unanticipated. The blame here is less mitigated than in the Jale' case by our Western tendency to hold the victim accountable because suicides can be thought of as especially vulnerable to messages that others might be expected to construe in harmless ways.

The point I would like to make here is that in these cases one sees a coming together of causation and blame. In the logic of traditional social science, the cause-effect relationship is essentially devoid of moral implications, the emphasis being on social—that is, nonindividual—causation, in which presumably the human actor is so far removed as to be out of the picture. In communication, however, a moral dimension is inevitable. The fact of human responsibility is unavoidable when the cause in question is a message. An agent is responsible for the message, whatever effects might have been intended or forseen, and at the same time, the effect takes place through the reading of the message, and another agent is responsible for that reading.

Emphasizing the human aspect—responsibility and blame rather than bare causation—represents one dimension in which communicative causation begins to diverge from causation in the traditional social sciences. Even in structuralism, although message is also central to questions of causation, elaborate measures have been attempted to remove questions of human responsibility. In the kind of structuralism practiced by Levi-Strauss, the author of the message disappears, and in Foucault's post-structuralism the reader is so reduced in options as to disappear also.

"UNSCIENTIFIC" FEATURES OF COMMUNICATIVE CAUSATION

In the standard, scientific conception of causation, cause and effect are sharply separated. A cause is an effect, but it is an effect of a previous cause. Likewise, an effect is the cause of a subsequent effect, but in the given causal sequence, the two are logically distinct (McIver, 1942). When a message is the cause of an effect, as I have argued, one must consider two human agents as parts of the sequence; a cause agent produces a message, and an effect agent reads or construes it. In order that the effect be produced, the effect agent must operate on the cause, in a sense recreating it simultaneously with the effect. This situation creates an interpentration of cause and effect that profoundly disturbs the mutual exclusivity of the two demanded by the logic of standard science.

Perhaps the most basic tenet of the traditional concept of causation concerns time. A cause must precede an effect. An effect cannot possibly come before its cause in sequential time. But here again when a message is looked upon as a cause, the traditional order becomes unrealistic. In social theory the structuralists, drawing upon the structural linguistics of Saussure, have explored another concept of time—synchronic time. Synchronic time, if it can be called time at all, collapses past, present, and future to form a single timeless dimension. The elements of a system such as language—the archetypal example—exist simultaneously, influencing one another to the extreme extent of creating one another's identity, but without priority or sequencing in time.

Synchronic time—in which causes and effects can go backwards, forwards, and sideways—is just as natural and commonplace to humans as diachronic or sequential time. One is the time of nature and the other the time of mind. We move freely between past, present, and future in our imaginations. In this sense the human present is constantly influenced by the future; a present effect is produced by a future cause. The past is also caused by the present, in this way of looking at things. A hundred years ago a philosopher or social theorist may have formulated a statement that I read for the first time today. This message is a cause that results in the effect of a change in my understanding of something. But this past cause is not the same now as it was when it was written. As I read it now in light of present knowledge and experience, the message is changed. The past cause is changed by what in its own terms is the future, and that future is to a degree the effect of the cause in question. I read Freud in light of a world that has been in some sense created by Freud. The cause is altered by the effect, which is of course impossible and backwards.

Everything I have just said can be, and usually is, stated in terms of sequential cause and effect and the time of nature. The present is not altered by the past because a person's idea of the future is not "really" the future at all. Instead, it is a present idea that has an effect on subsequent thought or action. Likewise the past I referred to is not really the past but a present idea of the past. My reading of Freud is a present effect caused by my previous experience.

Both of these alternative readings make sense in their own ways, but which is preferable? Natural science has rejected the first approach for a very good reason. If one applies the concept of causation and time associated with the human mind to nature, the result is pseudoscience. If an idea of the future is confused with the "real" future, prophesy or clairvoyance is postulated.

But when, as in communication, a message is considered a cause, the realm being explored is that of human interaction—culture—not that of nature. Just as applying the conceptions of time and causation of culture to the realm of nature results in a pseudoscience of nature, it can be argued that applying the conceptions of causation and time of nature to the realm of culture results in a pseudoscience of human interaction.

COMMUNICATION AND THE SEA CHANGE
IN SOCIAL SCIENCE

The objection to pseudoscience, of whatever topic, is that it appropriates the appearance of the scientific method, concentrating on a show of technique and paraphernalia, while it neglects the real questions it pretends to address. Worse, it doesn't work. Pseudoscience by definition is all promise and no result.

Critics of the dominant tradition in American social science have raised serious questions about its ability to answer the questions that a science of society ought to address (e.g., Giddens, 1976). While critics and alternate traditions of explanation have been around for a long time, the striking development in recent decades has been the pervasive character of a dissaffection that swept the social science disciplines.

When criticism crosses discipline lines in this way, it is clear that the underlying objection has to do with the common rather than the contrastive elements of the problematics of the sciences involved.[1] In the present case, I believe fundamental notions of cause and time that underlie the social sciences have been brought into question by a reformulation of the question that social scientists are asking.

---

[1] In their recent assessment of modern trends in ethnography, Marcus and Fischer (1986) underscore the importance of the idea that culture is essentially communication. Developments in current social theory also indicate an increasing centrality of the concept of communication; in Habermas the focus is explicit, as in his Theory of Communicative Action (1984), while Giddens' work on structuration theory (1979) strongly reinforces the primary character of the communication process. It can be argued that the investigation of communication can form the common ground for the coalescence of the artificially divided social sciences into that third, coequal branch of human knowledge—along with natural science and ethics—the "doctrine of signs" that Locke proposed in his *Essay Concerning Human Understanding* in 1690.

But does communication study have a sufficiently distinctive character to justify its being considered a discipline? Does it ask questions that other forms of social science do not ask, or does it ask its questions in a distinctive way? The fact that communication inquiry spans a number of existing disciplines does not in itself disqualify it as a distinct intellectual enterprise. The test, as Gluckman (1974) argues in her examination of structuralism, is whether the problematic of the field is different from those of others. Althusser defines the problematic as the underlying theoretical structure of a

Georgoudi and Rosnow comment that it is "no surprise that communication researchers are caught up in the contagion of unrest that
has spread through the social sciences" (1985, p. 76). The implication is
that they are participating because they are social scientists, and the
contagion has hit all social scientists equally. I would argue that while
the movement may not have originated among those identified by
discipline links with the field of communication research, the *topic* of
communication is in fact the point of origin. The question that
dissaffected social scientists are asking in all fields is precisely the
central question of communication: How does a message produce an
effect in social life? Gouldner, in his influential *The Coming Crisis of
Western Sociology* (1970), characterized Parsonian structural-func-
tionalism, the dominating social theory in the postwar era, as having
"solved" the problem of causality by ignoring it. Since "everything is
influenced by everything," social events are treated as not having
causes. Gouldner argued that this answer was so patently unacceptable that the problem of causation would reassert itself. It has done so
in a climate of social thought that is much more concerned with
meaning and discourse that was previously the case.

THE THREE WORLDS, THEIR REGIMES OF
CAUSATION, AND THEIR INTERRELATIONS

Peirce observes that the person lives in two worlds simultaneously: the
inner world of the imagination and the outer world of physical reality
(1955). Habermas, however, takes into account the difference between
the natural world, over which human will does not wield a determinative hand, and the intersubjective reality of the social realm, created

---

science that delimits the universe within which its problems can be posed. The
problematic sets the agenda for the field of study, and it does it in such an absolute way
that alternative conceptualizations are simply not possible. They are invisible and
unthinkable (Althusser & Balibar, 1979).

A problematic is complex and can be broken up into a number of elements. Ideas
about methods and scope of inquiry, as well as basic notions of ontology and epistemol-
ogy, can be blended in various ways, and the resulting combinations distinguish one way
of knowing and investigating from another. Related branches of science share many
basic elements, and a particular concept of causation, for example, is widely shared
among the social sciences. If one field were to have a distinctive way of looking at
causation, however, that would indicate its separate identity. I would argue that
communication, if it is to emerge as a distinct form of social inquiry, will diverge along a
path of causation partially explored by structuralism but largely invisible to traditional
empirical science.

by human interaction and understanding. For Habermas there is "my" world, "the" world, and "our" world, the inner, the outer, and the social worlds (1979).

The problem I have posed in this chapter—the question of relationship between, and particularly the lines of causation between, talk about conflict and the social practices that give rise to conflict—can be located in the social world, and the form of causation involved in understanding the problem is the specific kind of causation associated with that world. That kind of causation—which arises when a message is looked upon as a cause—is what I have called communicative causation, and it can be understood only in relationship to the forms of causation that characterize the other two worlds.

The inner world, the world of subjective reality, is normally so well coordinated with the outer world and the social worlds that the differences among them are unobtrusive; they are different but they are not at odds with one another. In an autobiographical account of his experience in a Nazi concentration camp, Viktor Frankl provides a dramatic example of the divergence between the two. Describing a forced march that was part of the daily routine of slave labor, he says:

> Almost in tears from pain (I had terrible sores on my feet from wearing torn shoes), I limped a few kilometers with our long column of men from the camp to our work site. Very cold, bitter winds struck us. I kept thinking of the endless little problems of our miserable life...
>
> I became disgusted with the state of affairs which compelled me, daily and hourly, to think only of such trivial things. I forced my thoughts to turn to another subject. Suddenly I saw myself standing on the platform of a well-lit, warm and pleasant lecture room. In front of me sat an attentive audience on comfortable upholstered chairs. I was giving a lecture on the psychology of the concentration camp! (1963, pp. 116–117)

Professor Frankl's lecture did not take place in the outer world and in fact was at odds with it, but it was just as real as his immediately preceding train of thoughts—concerning how to get a scrap of wire to use as a boot lace and whether his foreman for the day would be one of the brutal ones—which had been more in accord with what was actually happening to him. The possibility of complete divergence between what is going on in the inner world and the happenings in the outer and social worlds, as Frankl's book convincingly argues, is essential to the maintenance of human dignity and morality.

The reality and the importance of the inner world is easy to demonstrate, but what can be said of the patterns of causation that structure it? Freud's exploration of this realm provides great insight

WORLD	RESISTANCE	SCIENCE	DOMAIN	CAUSATION
Inner	Knowledge, Capacity to Think	Semiotics	Language System	Primary
Outer	Time, Space, Mass	Physics	Natural World	Physical
Social	Physical and Social Barriers	Ethno-graphy of Communi-cation	Communi-cation System	Communi-cative

Figure 2.1   The Three Worlds and their Regimes of Causation

along these lines, and his conceptualization can form the basis of the discussion (Figure 2.1).

Clearly the thoughts Frankel recounts—both of the lecture and the more "realistic" ones—correspond to the workings of the secondary process. Both trains of thought are under the control of the ego and quite effectively serve, each in its own way, the function of coping with the external realities. But I would argue that the regime of causation operant in the inner world is that of the primary process, which in the most fundamental sense is quite divorced from the external world. Conscious thoughts are keyed to the external world, but they are not bound by it. Thoughts of obtaining a scrap of wire later in the day are no closer to actually doing it than are thoughts of giving a lecture, regardless of the differences in probability of the events taking place in the outer worlds. Within that world itself, in which the two activities exist and have their realities, the resistance or constraint of time, space, and mass is totally absent. The person—that part of the person involved in this world—moves instantly between past, present, and future, from the horrors of the concentration camp to the plea-sures of the lecture hall. The constraints here are those of limits to knowledge and intelligence, not those of the physical and social worlds. Causation in this world is obviously different from that of the other worlds, and I would call it primary causation, with reference to Freud's (1953) delineation of the primary process.

If Freud can serve as a guide to the causation structure of the inner world, the whole body of philosophy associated with empirical science, from the Renaissance on, helps to delineate that of the outer, physical world. Bertrand Russell (1943) observes that no mature science accepts statements of causation of the simple form "A causes B" (and see von Bertalanffy, 1968, pp. 44–46). And yet, the complexities of multiple, mediating, contextual variables, feedback, and circular causation always boil down to an intricate network of "A causes B" relationships. The theoretical physicist Steven Hawkings, in his recent, popular *A Brief History of Time* (1988), shows the solid status of the one-way "arrow of time" in the analysis of any physical world that human could participate in.

Hume (1969) reduced the idea of causation to one of sequence, assuming that all knowledge must come from experience and that we can experience causation only as A happening and then B happening. We cannot know that A causes B or that the next time A happens B will happen. Of course we tend to think that we *do* know just that, but Hume shows that we are not logically justified in this, however practical such a way of thinking may prove to be in everyday life.

Hume's assertion that an unvarying experience of A then B "causes" us to believe that A causes B and that it will do so in the future indicates that he is treating the internal causation of the mind as something different from that of the outer world—otherwise he is assuming something about the workings of the very thing he is trying to define. I am proposing to follow this lead and assume that different kinds of causation prevail in the different worlds.

Heidegger (1962) discusses the problem of causation along traditional Aristotelian lines using a silver chalice as an example. What, he asks, is the cause of the chalice? Is it the physical impact of the workman's tools on the silver, or is it the idea of the chalice in his mind? This pre-Humean approach reintroduces the notion of goal or purpose into the discussion of causation. For our purposes, we might also postulate that an artist designed the object and a craftsman executed the design. Evidently there is something like a chain of events involved that includes processes of thinking, communication, and physical work.

Human causation—"A causes B" equated with "A happens and then B"—can describe the physical work, but other paradigms must be used for the other parts of the chain. The common thread, I would argue, is the idea of resistance or constraint. In describing the impact of the hammer and stake on the silver, we deal with constraints of distance, time, and mass. The precise nature of the dent depends on the weight and speed of the hammer, the direction in which it is wielded, and so on. If the hammer is too heavy or light, the force too great or too little, or the relative positions of the objects off target, the desired shape will not be produced.

But the notion of a desired shape returns us to the idea and the realm of the inner world. Here time and distance and mass are not constraints. As I have argued, knowledge and the capacity to deal with it are the major points of resistance in the inner world. And, if ideas are signs, as Locke, Peirce, and other semioticians argue, the mechanics of this world are described not by the physical laws of the outer world but by the laws governing the interactions of signs.

What we know about this realm of causation—in other words, the entire body of knowledge comprised by semiotics—must be brought to bear in understanding the part of the chain that has to do with the idea of the chalice, its origin and development, in the mind of the artist. One thing we know, for example, is the existence of the two dimensions that so many explorers of the inner world have encountered and described: Sausure's syntagmatic and paradigmatic (1966), Freud's similarity and contiguity (1953), Jakobson's selection and combination (1960), Pike's spot and class (1967), and so on. It seems clear also that signs exist not as individual items but only in complex interrelationships with other signs (Derrida, 1978) structured by the dimensions just cited into an infinitely extensible semantic field and ordered by a subjective sense of normality (Haas, 1960, 1964) built up by direct and indirect experience with the use of signs (Wittgenstein, 1967; Peirce, 1955). It is in this sort of landscape that processes of meaning, metaphor, and implication operate to define what I have called primary causation.

Moving to the third part of the problem—the communication of the idea for the chalice from the artist to the craftsman—one encounters the third world, that of social reality. Here, resistance is both physical—time and distance and problems with the transmission of signals have to be overcome if a message is to have an effect—and mental. But here the mental landscape is not continuous and confined to a single mind. All the well-recognized problems of misunderstanding and persuasion within a community add up to the barriers to intended effects that communicative causation must contend with.

Teleological explanation, in which the cause of an object or state of affairs is identified with the purpose it serves, has been seen as an anthropomorphization of nature. A motive or desired goal is projected without warrant into natural processes simply because we humans tend to have goals and to act on the environment so as to bring them about. Thus, a feature of society is explained by its service of a "societal need," or biological evolution is thought to be directed by a goal.[2]

---

[2] Burtt cites the argument that "the zenith of Greek metaphysics was attained quite consciously through the extension, to the physical realm, of concepts and methods already found helpful in dealing with personal and social situations," adding that "it is

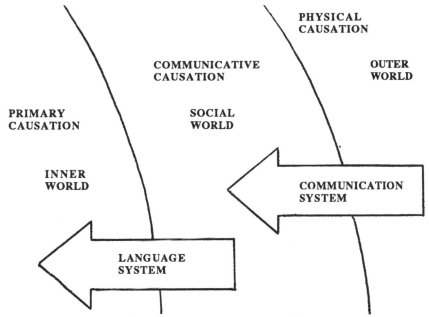

Figure 2.2   Interactive Origins and Domains of the Language and Communication systems

One can argue as well that the features of communicative causation represent an attempt to enforce desired characteristics of natural causation in the social world—a naturalization of culture. A cycle of reliance and compulsion, described in Chapter 6, creates an artificial and only partly successful Humean regime of "A, then B" where A and B are social acts. Absent rules and structures of enforcement, one could not really depend upon the sequence.

Clearly the three worlds and their causalities are interrelated and coordinated. Figure 2.2 shows how language and communication mediate among them. Language arises from the interaction of the inner and the social worlds. That is, the characteristics of the mind allow the development of language, a social artifact in the community. Language then invades and colonizes the mind. By this I mean that language furnishes the concepts and conventions of logic that govern

---

difficult for the modern mind, accustomed to think so largely in terms of space and time, to realize how unimportant these entities were for scholastic science," because "[i]nstead of spatial connexions of things, men were seeking their logical connexions; instead of the onward march of time, men thought of the eternal passage of potentiality into actuality" (1932, pp. 6-7).

perception and thinking, imposing limits at the same time as allowing the operations to take place. Thus Freud (1953) can argue that language creates and structures the secondary process or ego, allowing the conscious mind to engage in rational thought.

A parallel process takes place, I argue, at the interface between the social and outer worlds. Here what I call the communication system arises, based on the physical and linguistic potentials of the society as it interacts with the physical realities of the environment. And here again the system thus generated invades and colonizes, but it is the social world that is governed according to the constraints and possibilities thus created.

COMMUNICATION PATTERNS AND BARRIERS TO COMMUNICATION

A communication system in which there were no barriers to the flow of information and messages—even if such a system were possible—would have no shape or character. Barriers to communication are like the negative space in a picture or the ground to the figure; they establish the pattern, and the pattern can be manipulated by drawing lines—imposing restrictions—so that it responds to the needs of meaning and organizational function in the group.

Communication barriers are important in each of the three worlds delineated in this chapter. In the inner world of the mind and imagination, Freud's explorations have shown the tremendous significance of the barrier to communication between the unconscious and the conscious. The mechanism of repression—which can be seen as a restriction on the flow of ideas—in a sense creates the distinctive personality of the individual, channelling psychic energy, both positive and negative, into the meanings of the objects and concepts that constitute a person's mental life and powerfully influence his or her behavior and choices.

In the outer world, barriers to human communication are created by oceans, mountains, distances, time, and population densities. Just as Freud charted the barriers within the mind, examining their effects on behavior and character and exploring the therapeutic technologies that can be employed to reshape them, Harold Innes (1951, 1972) was a pioneer in analyzing the impact of natural communication barriers on the development of societies. From Innes's perspective, human history can be understood as the working out of the implications of the technologies that have been invented to reconfigure the barriers—from writing systems to the communications satellite.

Communication barriers in the social world are created by rules, and they represent a response to combined effects of the barriers presented by the other two worlds as they come together in the unique historical and ecological situation enjoyed by the particular society. Social barriers govern who can talk to whom about what, and they also determine the impact of a particular message on the individuals' behavior. They create regimes of authority, influence, and credibility. In the aggregate impact of their operation, they constitute the institutions that define the specific society.

The communication system on Yanuyanu island, perhaps more easily than would be the case in larger and more heterogeneous social situations, can be described concisely in terms of an internally consistent set of rules that govern how people interact. While there are alternate frameworks, either in competition or in complementary distribution, that operate to guide interaction, it is clear that there is one dominating system of rules on the island, and it is associated with kinship. The following three chapters present a sketch of the broad outlines of the kinship-based communication system on Yanuyanu. Chapters 3 and 4 describe the prescribed patterns of message exchange that structure the substance and meanings of everyday intercourse at the group-to-group level (Chapter 3) and at the individual level (Chapter 4). Chapter 5 concentrates on the critical problem of how the communication system evolves and sustains itself through conflict management. It is the framework created by this system of conflict management that constitutes the dominant regime of communicative causation on the island—the system whereby A causes B in the community when A and B are simultaneously messages and social acts.

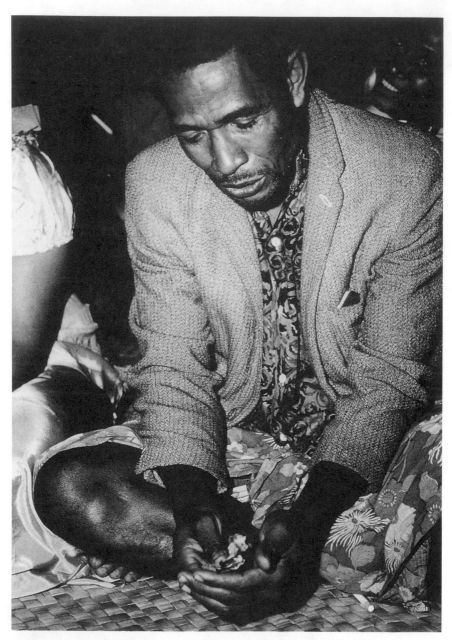

Spokesman for a Dance Troup Receiving with Ritual Speech and Gesture a Presentation of Money after a Dance Performance

3

The Communication System on Yanuyanu: Group-to-Group Interactions as Message Flow Patterns

"Just look at this. This is the kind of troublesome burden that women bring to a kin group."
  Husband, contemplating baskets of food
  prepared by his group as a contribution for
  the funeral feast of his wife's father's
  brother, addressing the ethnographer but
  glancing mischievously at his wife.

"What a tale! And where were these kinsmen obtained?"
  Wife, feigning outrage, then laughing.

(fieldnotes, June 28, 1972)

A WEDDING FEAST

On Yanuyanu, complicated, large-scale community events involving complex timing and the coordinated efforts of the whole village can be carried out faultlessly—and without the endless discussion and committee work that members of a small American community would have to endure—because people know what is expected of them and what to expect of others.

For example, during my stay on the island a traditional wedding took place that involved the division of the entire community into two ad hoc groups or sides: the bride's and the groom's. Participation on one side or the other carried specific obligations—contributions of goods, work, and performances toward the presentations that the one group would make to the other—as well as reciprocal rights to share in the presentation of goods and entertainments that would be returned.

The wedding, which was the first full-scale traditional celebration of this kind to take place in the village for 10 years, involved four days and nights of feasting, exchanges of valuables, and ceremonies. Most weddings in recent times have been much less elaborate, and the full-blown event is attempted only when both families want to demonstrate their importance. Preparations, which had to be started months ahead of time, included heavy planting and increased livestock production by both sides, as well as the construction of a new house and kitchen for the newlyweds near the groom's father's house. In addition, feasting facilities, including large, roofed eating pavilions, had to be set up both at the groom's and the bride's families' compounds.

On the morning of the first day, each side made two earth ovens to cook the large quantities of raw food brought by the participants. One oven was to cook lunch for the crowd that had gathered at each compound, and the other oven was to cook the feast that was to be presented to the other side later in the day. Each meal on each side had to serve two to three hundred people in generous style. After lunch a large procession left the bride's compound and carried a feast of cooked vegetables and pigs to the groom's compound. When everything had been piled up on display in front of the groom's pavilion, the result was a small mountain of fragrant baked yams, sweet potatoes, plantains, and pork, wrapped in broad green leaves and packed into freshly woven blankets.

At this point a spokesman for the bride's side made a speech presenting a whale's tooth to the groom's side. A representative of the chiefly family accepted on behalf of the groom's side with a few words, and then a ceremonial spokesman for the chief "finished" the acceptance with a longer speech. The spokesman for the groom's side then presented a "sending off" whale's tooth to a chiefly representative on the bride's side, who, like his counterpart on the other side, accepted with few words. The bride's side spokesman then finished up the acceptance for their side. Ceremonial clapping, *cobo*, marked each acceptance.

The pattern of reciprocity established here marked the entire four-day event. After the bride's side had returned to their compound, the groom's side carried a feast—this one featuring an entire cow—to the bride's side, where whale's teeth were again exchanged with appropri-

Figure 3.1.   Young Women Performing a Lauan Dance at the Wedding

ate speeches. Afterwards, women from each side paraded to the other carrying valuables such as stenciled barkcloth and mats. Later in the evening, at each compound, a spokesman called out the name of each household—or rather the name of its house foundation—participating on its side, and an assistant wielding a switch struck one of the many large baskets, woven of green palm fronds and lined up in the compound, packed with cooked food that represented each household's share of the feast that the other side had presented.

And all this was only on the first day. On the following three, with a day out for Sunday between the third and fourth, an equally intense schedule of activity took place. At two or three o'clock in the morning of the second day, the village was awakened by a band of mature women from the bride's side shouting, laughing, and banging pots, pans, and empty biscuit tins as they escorted the mother of the bride home from the newlyweds' house. They were celebrating the virginity of the bride, which had been proven to the satisfaction of both sides. A few hours later a large breakfast feast, called the "cock's crow" was taken to the bride's side with more clowning and potbanging, which is called *qirikapa*, "ringing metal."

A frequent type of exchange during the rest of the wedding was that of *meke*, group dance performances (Figure 3.1). Young women from

Figure 3.2.   Mature Women Dressed as "Indians" Perform a Comic Dance

each side danced while elder women and men provided accompaniment
by singing and playing instruments such as small slitgongs and large
sections of bamboo that produce a low, booming, organlike note when
struck on the ground. Alternatively, the young women formed the
orchestra while the older women danced.

The effect of the young women's dance was to show off their beauty
and grace, while the older women's dances were comic. On the fourth
day, for example, the matrons of the bride's side presented what they
called an Indian meke, *meke vakaidia*, to great hilarity (Figure 3.2).
The women wrapped themselves in white bed sheets, covered their
faces with flour, and balanced buckets and pots on their heads. Each
wore an exaggerated, fixed grin on her face—this is in contrast to the
Fijian style of dancing with a stoic expression—and they danced before
a woman seated on a large chair, who represented a fierce-looking
"sultan" attended by two guards with warclubs on their shoulders.
The sultan was played by the District Nurse, who was also the
choreographer; she said that she had learned the dance on the major
island of Viti Levu, where large numbers of Fiji Indians live.

The dancers, in both comic and straight performances, are rewarded with cries of encouragement and joking praise—"Oh! How fair she is! She looks like a woman of Hawaii!"—and by *fakawela*, in which audience members who are overcome with admiration dash out to dust them with scented talcum powder and shower them with sweets, cigarettes, and paper money. Young men often strip off their shirts and drape the dancers with them. Meanwhile, the dancers try to maintain their poker faces.

The atmosphere of the wedding, in other words, is one of good humor and generosity, and there is a great deal of clowning. On the morning of the third day I overslept and came late to the groom's compound, where I planned to join in the *yaqona* drinking, which was more or less continuous at both camps. As I sat down with a group of dignified elder men from the bride's side, I noted with complete surprise that, although carrying on exactly as usual, they were dressed as women. I was told that just previously the women of the groom's side had descended on them, oiling and powdering, to give them women's clothing to take home to their wives. The men, to show their *marau*, happiness, had put the dresses on over their own clothes.

On the morning of the fourth, final day, women from the bride's side came to the groom's compound to get her and escort her to the ocean for a ritual bath. Afterward, they took her fishing, and the fish they caught were to be used for a traditional feast. In this case, however, they caught so little that a pig had to be substituted. In the afternoon a large procession made its way through the village from the bride's compound to the groom's carrying household furnishings, including European-style furniture that the bride's father had received, just before the wedding, from woodworkers on Kabara island. They also carried a feast, and they presented everything with a whale's tooth and ritual speech. When they had received a whale's tooth in return, the bride's side presented two more whale's teeth, with more speeches. After two whale's teeth had been presented in return, and after a few more dance performances and many more rounds of *yaqona*, the event came to a close.

DECIDING WHICH SIDE TO TAKE

During and after the days of feasting and celebrations, I asked each head of household which side his family had gone to and why. In every case kinship provided the rationale for the decision. This is not to say, however, that kinship determined each choice. In some cases the strength of kin ties to one side or to the other made the decision obvious—close relatives of the groom's family went to his side, those of the bride's to hers. But in other cases a kin group might have less than overwhelming ties to either side, and logistical or political considerations could decide the issue.

To examine a particular instance, one large *i tokatoka*—which is a term for a group of closely related households that constitute a subunit within a *mataqali*, the landholding corporate group of Fijian society—comprised 11 households. Of these 11, 6 went to the bride's side, and 5 to the groom's. The decision as to who went where was made by the two most senior members of the *i tokatoka*, who were related as brothers to one another—because their fathers had been brothers—and as father to son to all the younger heads of households in the group. The father-son relationship does not imply actual parentage in each case; rather, it indicates the more general fact that the two men are one generation superior to the others among a group of men who are all descended through the male line from a single ancestor. In this case the most proximate such ancestor is the grandfather of the two elder members. Of these two elders, one is the acknowledged group leader by virtue of his father's having been the elder brother of the other old man's father.

These two decided to divide their forces in order to show their strength in both camps and also because they wanted to keep the two sides balanced for practical reasons—so that each side would have sufficient resources to carry out the exchanges.

When I asked each head of household within the *i tokatoka* about his participation on one side or the other, the reason given by those going to the groom's side was that their own and the groom's kinship units were very strongly related because "our fathers were brothers." In fact, the groom's father's father had been a member of their own *i tokatoka* who had married into another group and agreed to have his sons become members of their mother's kin unit. In genealogical terms, the younger household heads of the *i tokatoka* in question were related to the groom's father in that they had a common father's father's father's father, and two generations ago the families had all been in the same unit. One of the younger heads of household who went to the groom's side also justified his participation by saying that his wife and the groom's father were brother and sister on the female side—that is, their mothers were sisters.

The six who went to the bride's side said that they were not particularly well related to her group but that they were just following Cama, the second most senior member of their *i tokatoka*, who was going to the bride's side because his wife was the sister of the bride's father. She was not his sister in the strong sense of having the same parents but in a much more distant way. Actually, no one could specify the exact path except to say that she and he were from the same *mataqali*, although not from the same *i tokatoka* within it.

This example shows a pattern that prevailed throughout the community with regard to the wedding events: The constituent households of each kin unit acted in concert—even if in this one case the decision was to divide their support—based on the decisions of the leaders, and the decision was justified in kinship terms. By justification in kinship terms, I mean that the action was characterized as the fulfillment of an obligation created by a relationship. Why do I, my wife, and our children lend our support—yams, pigs, fish, stenciled barkcloth, performances as dancers or audience members, and so on—to the bride's group? Because Cama is my father, and that means I obey his wishes. Why does Cama support the bride's group? Because the bride's father is his wife's brother, his cross-cousin, and cross-cousins help each other when they are in need.

The relationship system at work here is, as I argued in the previous chapter, a communication system. On this island it is based on kinship, but that connection is as arbitrary as, in Saussure's terms, the connection between the sound of a word and the thing it stands for. In various societies or in various situations of social actions, a system that guides interaction might be based on religion, race, or capital—any set of interdependent roles and identities. The task I am proposing here is to explore the idea that such systems operate as communication systems—that is, they have their effect on social life by governing the pattern of message flow within the community.

Like a language, a communication system enables messages to be sent, but it does not entirely determine what the particular message will be. Operating within it, the "speaker" can create an original expression, as long as he or she observes the conventions of shared meaning within the group. And the expression, considered as the product of the communication system—not just as language or other meaningful action independent of the relationships among the speakers and hearers—is not one of representation, as in language. Rather, as I have argued, it is politics and economics. Malinowski (1923, p. 312) argued that language in a primitive society is a "mode of action" rather than an "instrument of reflection." I believe this makes sense only if we mean by it that a communication system—in any group—is a mode of action, and that language is almost always observed in the operation of a communication system. The two should not be collapsed analytically, however. Language itself is not a mode of action anywhere, and the communication system is a mode of action in every kind of society.

THE WEDDING AS A COMMUNICATION EVENT
AT THE GROUP LEVEL

Returning to the wedding, it is clear that the decision to act taken by the two leaders of the *i tokatoka* could have gone in many directions, and whatever they decided to do would be read by the rest of the community as a message about individual and group relations. Based on my discussions and observations in the community before and after the event, I present a partial gloss of their actions as an example of my general point that the transfer of valuable objects and performances, for example, *is* politics and economics within the group, but only by virtue of the *meaning* associated with the transfer. The transfer is a message, in other words (and in other than words), and my comments are meant as possible readings of it, not as a description of the reasoning processes or logic followed by the old men.

As it happens, the reader has already met two of the principal actors involved here. The senior leader of the *i tokatoka* is the person I called Epi in the case described in the first chapter, and the father of the bride is Vesu, the owner of the cow that damaged Epi's garden. (And the cow was the one featured in the wedding feast, that being the reason for its being raised by Vesu in the first place.)

In causing damage to Epi's property, and in then failing to perform the ritual apology, *i soro*, in which he would have acknowledged his fault and his obligation of obedience to Epi as a son to a father, Vesu had portrayed himself as independent of the old man. Afterall, he was a mature man himself with sons of his own; he commanded two younger brothers, both married men with children, and the three households constituted the core membership of a social unit separate from Epi's—not only a different *i tokatoka* but a different *mataqali* in a different village, due to his father's shift of descent lines. From the point of view of blood, Vesu was clearly subordinate to Epi, but from the point of view of corporate group membership Vesu was clearly autonomous. Vesu's behavior showed that he emphasized the latter, but Epi was prepared to insist upon the former way of reckoning the relationship.

Epi was now in a position to rebuke Vesu, perhaps even to bring him to heel. By denying his support, or by minimizing it, he could make Vesu's son's wedding much less effective as a demonstration of Vesu's economic power and social influence. On the other hand, Epi was also in the position to demonstrate his superior conformity to the higher ideals of Fijian traditions. In supporting Vesu he could demonstrate the depth of his understanding that the relationship at stake, as in every interpersonal conflict on the island, was the relationship between two groups (or categories within a group), not between individuals who might have some petty quarrel. This, of course, would make Vesu look even meaner in comparison.

Providing equally powerful support for the bride's group made a dramatic statement of the centrality of Epi's group and its benevolent dominance in the community at large. This kind of message would be read by the village in light of a contest for leadership that was in progress at the time. The paramount chief of the island had died, and it was not clear who would succeed him. One faction supported the claim of the old chief's daughter, and they recognized her as chief. Their theory was that she should take the office as the eldest survivor of the senior chiefly line.

Epi's group had a different theory. They argued that Epi was the chief because he represented the line descended from the younger son of the original "conquering" chief who had founded the present line. This chief had led the island into the political orbit of the chief of Lakeba, the Tui Nayau, who eventually gained control of all of Lau. The Tui Nayau, in fact, had been his father, although his mother was from an indigenous chiefly family of the island.

Epi's reading of island history and tradition was that the true pattern of succession was one of alternation between senior and junior lines within the chiefly family. As leader of the junior branch, it was now his turn to be installed. A third position, which ultimately triumphed, was that the eldest son of the old chief's brother had the strongest claim, given that he was the oldest *male* representative of the senior chiefly line. None of these claimants could win out, however, until he or she had been installed with the appropriate traditional ceremony, the *veibuli*, by the community. Here the nonchiefly social units—the "land", *vanua*, as they are referred to—felt that they held the trump card. Only they could perform the *veibuli*, and without it no one was chief.[1]

The bride's group, as it happened, was of the land. Epi's decision to support the bride's group restated the alliance between his chiefly group and the land he hoped to lead—once properly installed as chief—with the benevolence and mutual respect portrayed metaphorically by this gesture of generous support.

---

[1] As discussed below, this theory of the relationship of the *vanua* to the *turaga* is not undisputed. Historical accounts by both Hocart (1929) and Thompson (1940) describe a regional system in which the chiefs of the vassal islands are selected and installed by the paramount chief of Lau, the Tui Nayau. In the instant case, the candidate who was finally installed—with the full participation by the *vanua* but not that of the junior branch of the chiefly line—was the choice of the encumbent Tui Nayau.

Unfortunately, Epi's junior branch of the chiefly line was not universally perceived as exemplifying those particular civic virtues. They were a very numerous group, having grown while some of the other descent groups had declined in size. These other groups, with only a few people but with large amounts of land, felt somewhat vulnerable. Epi's group threatened to outgrow its allotted share of the island's land, and its members were accused of pursing an aggressive program of planting trees to establish permanent claims to land that should be used only by permissions of other groups.[2] Furthermore, an aura of arrogance and a tendency to resort quickly to physical violence were ascribed by some to Epi's family. Arrogance and violence are chiefly attributes too, but they are not among those cherished by the land in times of peace.

This kind of consideration points to another reason for Epi's support of Vesu. The very fact that Vesu's father had left the group that Epi now heads and had arranged for his sons to be members of their mother's *mataqali* rather than his own is indicative of the imbalance of land and group size that had begun to show up on the island. Vesu's mother's father had no sons, and he was the leader of a group that seemed to be threatened with extinction. He decided, therefore, with the consent of all concerned, to treat his daughter's three sons as his own. Now, long after the old man's death, some of the other members of the *mataqali* did not agree that Vesu and his brothers really belonged to the group. They were saying that the brothers' rights to cultivation in *mataqali* land were derived only from their mother—they had only the relationship of *vasu* to the group—and their rights would end with their mother's death and could not be passed on to their own children. It was reported that some had used the phrase "*e ratou sa ravi tiko qa*," "they are only leaning here." In other words, they lacked a *yavu*, a foundation that could be built upon. Under these circumstances, Vesu and his brother represented an outpost of the chiefly family that needed support if it were to retain its toehold in the rich and largely empty lands of their adoptive *mataqali*. Having strong kin links with people in that group—if they could be maintained as members—would represent a distinct advantage to an overpopulated *i tokatoka* such as Epi's.

---

[2] Gaining long-term control over land by planting trees would be an effective strategy only within a *mataqali*. In this case, the other *i tokatoka* within the chiefly *mataqali* were complaining about the tree planting activities of the junior branch of the chiefly family. The temporary use of garden lands controlled by other *mataqali*, however, is easy to obtain from sympathetic kinsmen within it. A person has especially well-defined and secure rights to the use of the lands of his or her mother's *mataqali*.

It made sense, therefore, for Epi's group to support both sides strongly. In so doing, however, they did not want their actions to be read as indicating internal division. Epi himself went to the groom's side, and the other elder member of the *i tokatoka*, Cama, who is treated with almost equal respect in the group and who had formerly held a high government post, went to the bride's group, citing the tie through his wife. Epi's elder son went with Cama, while the younger joined him. Epi's daughter, who is married to a man from a neighboring island and whose household is treated as a part of Epi's kin unit, went with Cama, as did Cama's own son. Another set of two brothers divided themselves also, one to each side, and among the other three brothers in the *i tokatoka*, one went to the bride's side and two to the groom's.

Kinship, then, as a system of relationships among individuals and groups on the island, did not determine the actions of the people involved, but it did provide the medium in which the statements constituting the social process could be articulated. Its potential stretches well beyond the shores of the island, and marriages are seen as a means of extending its reach, giving the kin unit in question a "long arm" for reaching out to wealth and power over a large area. In the wedding just described, for example, the father of the bride found it easy to obtain furniture and other wooden goods from Kabara in exchange for goods produced on Yanuyanu because three wives in his *mataqali* had come from Kabara.

While I lived on the island, there was also an active exchange network involving Epi's group and people on the island of Oneata. Men and women sailed back and forth in both directions—using traditional outrigger canoes obtained in exchanges with specialized craftsmen on the wooded islands such as Kabara, Fulaga, and Ogea—giving one another pigs, cows, garden products, canoes, and other objects of material and ceremonial wealth. But this exchange network was not the automatic result of kinship links or customary practices. Rather, the activity was specifically initiated in the 1930s and 1940s by Epi and Cama. At that time their group had no active ties with Oneata, but Epi and Cama, then ambitious younger members of the group, could see that exchange with such a rich island would be highly desirable. In order to express their plan, they based their rights to engage in exchange on the fact that their common grandmother, their fathers' father's wife, had been a woman from Oneata.

Actually, she herself had been born on Yanuyanu, but her mother had come from Oneata and had married into one of the land *mataqali*. On the basis of this rather tenuous path of kinship, they and their wives had initiated a series of visits and *volau*, ceremonial exchanges, such as expeditions to "see the grave," *raibulubulu*, of relatives whose funerals they had not attended. They could have as easily chosen to forget about the kinship ties to Oncata, but instead they asserted them, and over the years the reactivated relationship continued to grow in volume of economic discourse.

GROUP-TO-GROUP PATTERNS: THE TURAGA AND THE VANUA

Having plunged the reader into the complexities of the relationship system, much as the ethnographer is immersed in it immediately without first seeing the stark simplicity of its larger outlines, I will describe the fundamental relationships that provide the idiom of social action at personal and group levels, beginning with the ways that one group is expected to interact with another.

The one pattern of relationship that pervades every institutional arrangement on the island is that of hierarchy (Figure 3.2). For

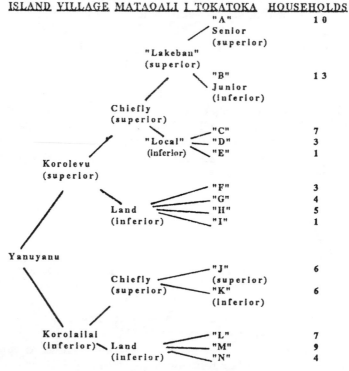

Figure 3.2.   Hierarchy among Groups on Yanuyanu

example, although they are contiguous on the ground, there are two villages on the island, and one is superior in rank to the other. Superior rank is often expressed in terms of chiefly, *turaga*, status as opposed to that of land, *vanua*, and the larger of the villages, which we can refer to as Korolevu, is *turaga* with respect to the smaller, Korolailai.

Within each village, also, the *turaga/vanua* opposition is represented; each village has a chiefly and a land *mataqali*. When the villages act independently, each has chiefly and land contingents to carry out the ceremonial and practical roles required by the event. When the two act together, however, the chiefly *mataqali* of the superior village takes precedence and carries out the chiefly role.

The pattern of hierarchical ranking also extends to relationships internal to the *mataqali* one *itokatoka* is superior and takes the leadership role in all common activities. The leader of this ruling *i tokatoka* is also the *pule*, or head of the *mataqali* as a whole. In theory, each of the other *i tokatoka* has a clearly defined rank in descending order. Ranking at this level of organization is possible because of a principle of heritable seniority based on order of birth. When households whose heads all trace descent from a single male ancestor become numerous enough, they may split off from their existing group and form a new *i tokatoka*. The rank of that new entity will be determined by the rank of its founding ancestor   it will be superior to those *i tokatoka* tracing ancestry to individuals junior to him, and inferior to those whose ancestors in his generation were his senior.

A series of titles, with defined relationships to one another, expresses functional roles among the *mataqali*. For example, the chiefly *mataqali* controls the title of paramount, or island chief. The chief is served by sort of executive officer, the *matanivanua*, one of whose jobs is to make ceremonial speeches on behalf of the chief in ritual situations.

As an example of the ritual relationship involved and of the flexibility with which the pattern is overlaid upon a variety of situations, I will refer back to an incident in the wedding described earlier. When the bride's side brought their feast to the groom's, it was presented with a whale's tooth and a ritual speech by Takelo, the *matanivanua* of island, whose *mataqali* belongs to Korolevu, the bride's village.

Accepting for the groom's side was Epi, the highest ranking "chief" among them. Epi's *matanivanua* for the occasion was Kirikiti, who is the regular *matanivanua* for Korolailai, the groom's village. Kirikiti then presented the return whale's tooth to Tiko, who was the highest ranking member of the island's chiefly *mataqali* present on the bride's side, and Takelo again acted as the *matanivanua* for him.

When the groom's side paraded from Korolailai to Korolevu to present the return feast to the bride's side, Epi and Kirititi were again the chief and the *matanivanua* for their side, but this time Cama, Epi's brother who had gone to the bride's contingent, was the chief for the bride's side; Takelo was again their *matanivanua*.

In other words, whenever two groups interact in exchange, even if the groups are *ad hoc*, synthetic ones, it is an interaction between two *turaga* acting through their *matanivanua*. In a pinch anyone can serve in either capacity, depending upon who else is present and who might have a better claim to the role. In terms of the theoretical argument of this chapter, the exchange or other ritual is a communication event as well as an exercise in politics and economics, and the part of the island communication system represented by the *turaga* and *vanua* relationships among groups guides what people will say and do—and what that saying and doing will mean—in the event.

The land *mataqali* of Korolevu owns the title of *matanivanua* of the island, and Takelo is the present incumbent. When he dies or retires from the position, his *i tokatoka* will decide who among them will take up the title. The land *mataqali* also owns the title of *bete*, or high priest, an office that comes into play only rarely today, as in the performance of a pre-Christian ritual such as the *veibuli* of a new chief. These constitute the dominant set of titles on the island, but, as noted earlier, the inferior village, Korolailai, also has a chief, who comes from the *turaga mataqali* of that village, and a *matanivanua* to serve him, in this case Kirikiti, who comes from the land *mataqali* of Korolailai.

REGIONAL SOCIAL THEORY AND LOCAL HISTORY:
A COLLISION OF DISCOURSES

These principles of hierarchical organization, the distinction between the *turaga* and land groups and the inheritance of seniority based on order of birth, form a largely agreed-upon basis for ordering relationships among the *mataqali* and among the *i tokatoka* within each *mataqali*. The traditional titles, and the rights and duties that attach to them, symbolize and personify the intergroup relations within the community. The clarity of this ordering framework—that is, the consensus it evokes—however, is largely due to its theoretical character. When it is actually put into operation, it collides with history, and the interaction of these two forms of village discourse insures that virtually every point of social organization is debatable. The debate it engenders, in fact, is the conflict dimension of the political and economic process of the village—the legitimation struggle over the allocation of wealth and power.

The *turaga/vanua* relationship is accepted in the abstract, for example, but the question of who among the island residents are the *turaga* and who are the *vanua* demands historical justification. The chiefs of Korolailai, for example, claim to be descended from an indigenous ruler who was the paramount chief of the island before it "went" to Lakeba—that is, became a political subordinate of Lakeba island. This explains why they are chiefs today within their own village and why they are subordinate to the island chief.

The subject relationship with the Tui Nayau, paramount chief of Lakeba, as mentioned above, came about with the installation of the Tui Nayau's son as chief of Yanuyanu. The takeover may not have been entirely hostile because the mother of this Lakeban chief was from an indigenous chiefly lineage of Yanuyanu. Her mataqali, however, was not that of the Korolailai chiefs, but another group, whose descendants are now a subdivision of the chiefly *mataqali* of Korolevu. (That is the *i tokatoka* headed by Tiko, who acted a chief for the bride's side in the absence in their group of any senior member of the "Lakeban" chiefly family such as Epi or Cama.)

The first "Lakeban" chief of the island had two sons, the elder of whom succeeded him as chief and was the founder of the senior branch of the chiefly line on Yanuyanu. When he died, the title went not directly to his son but to his younger brother, and when the younger brother died—thus exhausting the superior generation of the line—the title went to the son of the elder brother as the highest ranked of his generation. The meaning of this sequence is a matter of debate and interpretation. One view is simply that the chiefs from that time to this have come from the senior branch of the family. In this view the two sons of the original chief are seen as members of the same line: when the senior died, the title went to the next most senior, but when the title descended to the next generation, it went to the son of the elder of the brothers, who was senior to the sons of the younger. The other version of history retrospectively emphasizes the fact that the younger brother of the second chief was the founder of the junior chiefly line, now headed by Epi. According to this reading of history, the succession from elder brother to younger brother and then to the elder brother's son should be read as an alternation between two lines: from senior to junior and then back to senior.

Laura Thompson (1940), in her account based on ethnographic research in the 1930s, presents a version of chiefly succession on Yanuyanu that is consistent with the regional perspective from Lakeba. In it, there is only one chiefly line on Yanuyanu, and it is the one descended from the first Lakeban chief. Since his time, all chiefs have come from the senior branch of the family. All other *mataqali* on the island are of the land. From this regional perspective, too, it is clear that the Tui Nayau, who is chief of Lakeba and paramount chief of Lau, has historically played the role of selecting the chiefs to be installed in his vassal islands.[3]

This version of history was advocated in some degree by one faction in the succession controversy going on during my visit; those who supported the son of the old chief's brother—rather than the chief's own daughter, or Epi as the pretender from the junior line—saw him as the preferred candidate of the encumbent Tui Nayau.

This line of argument has a number of important implications for group-to-group relations on the island. For one thing, it takes away what I have referred to as the land groups' trump card—their power to select the new chief by refusing to install any candidate they did not approve. Casting that relationship between the *turaga* and the *vanua* in regional rather than strictly local terms weakens the *vanua*, pitting them not against the local chiefs alone but against the Tui Nayau, a figure of great traditional and contemporary political power.

The broad, regional view, which ignores the kind of local deviation from the norm that would result in the alternation of chiefly succession between several lines, also threatens the local status of the chiefly *mataqali* of Korolailai. Their claim to indigenous chiefly status is supported by a history that describes the transition of the island chieftainship in the pre-Lakeban era from one indigenous *mataqali* to another and then back again.

The general idea of the subordination of the *vanua* to the *turaga* group is well entrenched in island politics, but the basic character of the relationship can still be a topic of debate. Drinking *yaqona* with the *vanua*, I heard theories that portrayed the *turaga* as what

---

[3] Yet another faction in the succession controversy may be mentioned here, although it was a minor faction consisting of perhaps two brothers and their families within the chiefly mataqali. They embraced the theory of the Tui Nayau's power to install their chief, maybe because they had no other support, and wrote to him suggesting that the elder of the two be installed. They were not successful, and others took the occasion to explain that the branch of the chiefly line they claimed to represent was actually extinct—*kawa boko*, (Note here the use of the term *kawa*, a blood line, contrasted in the next chapter with the term *yavusa*. *Boko* means extinguished, as of a dead fire, or of the eyes as in *mataboko*, blind.) And that they were merely the descendants of an illegitimate member. Epi's group recognized that the Tui Nayau might intervene against them, but they argued that the situation resembled one in a neighboring island in which the intervention of the Tui Nayau was not effective in the face of division within the local chiefly *mataqali*.

amounted to servants of the land people. Some argued that "their time is over"; that is, the chiefs were useful in the era of interisland warfare, but now their former functions have been taken over by the government. From this point of view, the land people's rights to the island resources are primary and derive from their indigenous status. The chiefs are seen as outsiders who reside there by invitation and an implied continuing permission.

Yaqona sessions among the chiefly, however, yielded very different arguments. The land people are castigated as ingrates who ignore their duties towards the chief—such as bringing him all turtles and certain fish that should be reserved for his use—until they find themselves in need of the chief's protection and help.[4]

Another debatable dimension of group-level relations concerns the principle of inherited seniority that determines the rank of the *i tokatoka* within *mataqali*. Here again the historical reality of group formation provides great flexibility of interpretation. Every *mataqali* contains certain *i tokatoka* whose origins and relationships to the others can be challenged. For example, a man from another island or another *mataqali* on the island might reside with his wife's group for a variety of reasons. The children are considered part of the wife's group, but their status, and that of their descendants for many subsequent generations, is less than totally secure. Descendants of an illegitimate child within the group are also considered somewhat outside the system of seniority. People in such categories have every advantage of group membership, and their everyday lives are indistinguishable from those of the others except for one thing; in terms of the usual metaphor, they can never have a strong voice in the group. The longer the line resides within the *mataqali*, however, the stronger its voice grows, and the story of its origin must be kept alive by continual retelling among the members of the rival *i tokatoka* if they are to maintain their dominance.

Just as debate about social relationships among the groups on the island can be kept creatively flexible by the tension between local history and indigenous political theory, alternate theories can also be played off against one another. For example, kin links through women are honored as creating ties of obligation and entitlement, even though the line of descent through males normally determines group membership. The intervention of the government is also an important factor in some cases because the colonial administration's land commission

---

[4] Elsewhere (Arno 1979a), I have described cases that illustrate the institutionalized conflict between the *turaga* and the *vanua*.

hearings rearranged the *mataqali*, taking segments from some that were too large and placing them in other, smaller ones. When that happened, however, the traditional ties of descent remained in place, creating an alternate path of association. An incident that took place in the village several months after the big wedding illustrates some of the complications of intergroup relationships that arise in this complex system of overlapping frameworks.[5]

The incident involved Suka, a member of the chiefly *i tokatoka* headed by Epi, and his wife Meri, who was a member of an *i tokatoka* called Daligabuli within one of the land *mataqali*. Meri's father, Mo, had died in 1970. Throughout their marriage, Suka had shown himself anxious to cultivate ties with his wife's descent group; he had performed the ritual presentation of wealth called *vakalutulutu* in order to underscore his children's rights with respect to their mother's descent group's property. Suka had been on good terms with his father-in-law, Mo, who had been the leader of the Daligabuli group, and he also got along well with Eroni, Mo's brother, who had succeeded to leadership on Mo's death. In 1971 Eroni himself died, and the new leader was Loa, Eroni's eldest son.

About a year after Mo's death, the Daligabuli group made preparations for a ritual of commemoration for him called *dranukilikili*, which involves spreading small black pebbles coated with perfumed coconut oil over the grave of the person memorialized. The *dranukilikili* is a variety of *volau* or ritual exchange, and its important economic feature is a large-scale exchange between the relatives of the deceased who reside locally and a group of other relatives who live elsewhere. In this case, the Daligabuli group expected a group from Suva, and this meant they could anticipate receiving large amounts of cloth, soap, money, kerosene, and other town goods in exchange for their own traditional products such as barkcloth.

Suka decided to demonstrate his solidarity with Daligabuli by contributing to the food and barkcloth that would be presented. Because Suka's family contributed to the Daligabuli presentation, they would receive a proportionate share of the return presentation from the Suva group. Suka planned to convey his family's contribution to the site of the ritual in a small procession to be led by his daughter, who would be dressed in barkcloth and flower garlands; the purpose of this gesture would be to reaffirm the reciprocal obligations between the girl and her mother's agnates.

---

[5] I describe this case in an earlier article (Arno 1979a), in which I discuss ritual as a way of dealing with conflicts that are inherent in a form of social organization.

On the morning of the *volau*, a wave of talk swept through the chiefly group to the effect that Loa did not want Suka and his family to participate in the ritual. Members of Epi's group speculated that it was the women of Daligabuli who were behind the rebuff. The reason was said to be that they did not want to share the goods that were to be received from the Suva group. Epi and Cama, the leaders of the chiefly *i tokatoka*, decided that their entire descent group should attend the *dranukilikili*, and that their presentation should be especially generous, so as to put the Daligabuli people to shame.

The procession through the village was impressive; the men carried heavy baskets of food on poles balanced over their shoulders, and two lines of women carried, spread out between them, a large sheet of decorated barkcloth. Suka's daughter marched at their head, and when the contribution had been deposited in a large heap at the ritual site, Cama, the fiery-tempered second-in-command of the group began a formal presentation speech.

After beginning the speech in the usual way, he subjected the people of Daligabuli to a vigorous scolding. He began by saying, "I have heard that some of you did not want us to come here. Well, know this: no living person can break the bonds of kinship that unite our two groups." He went on to remind his audience that the founder of his group was also the ancestor (although through an illegitimate and therefore inferior line) of the man whose descendants form the group now known as Daligabuli. He recalled that the groups had lived together as one for many generations, and that their current separation was due to an administrative decision by the government land commission. He admonished them not to forget their origins and assured them that the bonds of blood are not easily broken.

The people of Daligabuli responded warmly to the speech, and later the members of Epi's group congratulated themselves on the way they had handled the problem. They assumed that the trouble was over-with, but soon after it appeared that Loa, the new leader of Daligabuli, and his followers wanted to evict Suka from a plot of land called Baniu, which had been given to Suka's wife by her father, Mo. Loa's argument was that the land belonged to Daligabuli as a group, and that they retained the power to say whether Suka might continue to use it or not.

Loa brought the matter before the *bosenivanua*, a neo-traditional island council headed by the paramount chief and including elders from each of the descent groups. As the office of chief was still vacant, Epi presided. A number of old men who were considered experts in matters of land tenure discussed the question, and their recommendation was that Suka be allowed to keep using the land.

The *bosenivanua* has no direct power to enforce its decisions but relies instead upon the persuasion of the elders to bring the disputants into agreement. In this case Loa decided not to accept their recommendation but wrote to the government agency in charge of Fijian lineage-held lands, asking that his group be certified as the owner of the land. After some time, the agency replied that the land in question was considered a *kovukovu*, a nonconforming estate within the larger segment belonging to Suka's chiefly mataqali. Although the land did not belong to Suka's *mataqali*, and therefore was not available for his use as a matter of birthright, neither did it belong to Loa's *mataqali* as a group. As a *kovukovu*, it had belonged to Mo personally, and he had been able to convey a life estate to his daughter. Suka's use of the land was thus confirmed.

In one sense, this case was about a struggle between two individuals, Suka and Loa. At a more fundamental level, however, it also represented an ongoing conflict, inherent in the necessary process of group fission that operates to adjust the balance between group size and land allocation over the generations, between the two social units involved. In that process, ritual events can be seen as a specialized, regulatory mode of communication about the state of group relationships.

The *dranukilikili* serves as an excellent illustration of the way that ritual statements—which are far from being absolutely prescribed in every detail of performance—can be articulated in a variety of ways so that the nuances of intergroup relations can be debated by those performing them. Suka's idea of giving his daughter a highly visible role was a specific statement, as of course was Loa's attempt to curtail the other group's participation and Cama's massive retaliatory rebuttal expressed both through expanded participation and his own speech.

In order to escape from—or at least to loosen—the smothering hierarchical embrace of the dominant group and establish itself as a relatively autonomous social unit, Loa's *i tokatoka* attempted to redefine the relationship not by denying the principle of hierarchy but, working within the idiom of the relationship/communication system in place, by appealing to higher levels of authority, first at the island and then at the national levels.

In looking at this conflict case from the group perspective, it is necessary to consider the extent to which the actions and verbal statements of individuals such as Suka, Loa, and Cama can be considered as authored by the group rather than the person. A reasonably long-term participant-observer in the groups would note, as I did in this instance, a continual stream of discussion, structured by the channels of normal, everyday communication in the groups, about the fundamental issues. Ritual actions and public speeches by the leaders do not just come out of the blue but are related—in ways that define the particular character of leadership in the group at the time—to this discourse.

For example, the men and women in Suka's group were right to point out the role of the women of Loa's *i tokatoka* in the move to exclude them. In saying this, of course, they were not making observations about the social process but instead were attempting to discredit the idea because the women of any such group are "merely" married into it—their own descent lines are elsewhere. Who are *they*, in other words, to talk about internal matters of descent. This polemical dimension aside, however, it is accurate to observe that rituals such as the *dranukilikili* belong to and are controlled by the women of the groups involved. Obviously the women of Daligabuli would have a very large voice in such matters.

The strength of the women's voice—their level of authority and control—was evident when another *dranukilikili* took place in the village, and I asked the male informant who had told me that it would be coming up if he would go with me to tape record and photograph certain of the exchanges. These particular exchanges were events that would take place in the house of leader of the host group before the more public rituals at the grave. My informant responded with considerable enthusiasm that he would be delighted to go with me. As we talked about it more over the next few days, he said that men never attended such exchanges and had no idea what went on in them except what their wives told them later. He said that he was very curious about the matter and greatly welcomed the opportunity, under the cover of legitimacy provided by my research, to learn about this part of Fijian custom.

When the morning of the exchange came, however, he deserted me at the door of the house. He explained that he didn't feel comfortable about going in. He said he really didn't know these women very well. Perhaps if they were closer relatives within his own *yavusa*, kindred,[6] he could talk to them. Instead, he went to join the men of the descent group who were drinking *yaqona* in a nearby house with the husbands of the visiting women. The women in the house welcomed me in, however, and they seemed to consider my activities an interesting, rather amusing elaboration of the event. I had sought their permission earlier, and I was told that they would be glad to have me and that they looked forward to listening to the tapes later.

---

[6] The important concept of the *yavusa* will be discussed in the next chapter, as it lends itself to an individual-centered analysis.

Ceremonial Clapping during a Ritual Presentation

4

The Communication System:
The Regulation of Message Flow
Among Individuals on Yanuyanu

> My great-aunt, speaking in a loud voice, to set an example, in a tone that
> she endeavoured to make sound natural, would tell the others not to
> whisper so; that nothing could be more unpleasant for a stranger coming
> in, who would be led to think that people were saying things about him
> which he was not meant to hear;...
>
> Marcel Proust, 1924 *Remembrance of Things Past*

Rituals such as the *dranukilikili* and the wedding, described in the
previous chapter, and others associated with death, birth, and marriage, reveal very clearly that the patrilineal groups I have emphasized so far in discussing social organization on the island—the
mataqali and *i tokatoka*—are not the only kind that are important.
People on either side of the various kinds of ritual exchanges come
together because they share group bonds, but the groups are not
patrilineally determined. In fact, they are defined very flexibly, and
several paths may be open to the individual. In many conversations
about kinship, informants stated that there are two sets of groups:
kawa and *yavusa*.

Unfortunately for present purposes of exposition, people use the
terms in different ways.[1] But although the terms are at times reversed

---

[1] Sahlins (1962) provides a full discussion of the variety of terms used in Fiji to talk
about kin units, and he documents the characteristic flexibility that villagers display as

in application, there is agreement about the basic difference between the two types of groups. One type, which many people refer to by the term *kawa*, is defined as a blood line. For example, the *kawa turaga* would be the people in the patrilineal descent group that own the title of island paramount. Within such a group, however, there are a number of *yavusa*, which are groups of cooperating, interdependent relatives. A *yavusa* includes patrilineal relatives—but not all of them—and also relatives through marriage. Both husbands and wives and the close relatives of both can be said to be *yavusa vata*.

The descendants of an animal or plant can be called its *kawa*, which is an important concept in breeding domestic animals. The term *yavusa*, however, would have no application here. The *yavusa* is an essential support group that a person in need—for example, because of the food and ceremonial objects of wealth demanded by a ritual related to death or marriage—can call upon. The *mataqali* and the *i tokatoka*, therefore, are only part of the story. As patrilineally defined descent groups, they are crucial in legalistic, exclusionary contexts such as reckoning the ownership of land. The *yavusa*, however, is inclusionary and is defined by participation in the activities of everyday life.

Yavusa structure appears to involve a dense core of obligation centered around a person or extended family.[2] Depending on circumstances, the *yavusa* expands to the size required, but the periphery is characterized by less intense networks of obligation. In the big wedding described above, both the bride's and the groom's families depended heavily on their core *yavusa*—not their *i tokatoka* or *mataqali*, although there may have been considerable overlap in memberships—and the large groups that ultimately participated on each side can be thought of as extended, situationally defined *yavusa*. Because of the overlapping and partly subjective character of the *yavusa*, the individual level of analysis brings them into focus.

---

contrasted with the official government definitions. With regard to the term *yavusa*, he says it "usually refers to people of one origin or descent—the descent at issue may strictly patrilineal...; or I have heard *yavusa* applied where descent was nonunilineal; or in reference to egocentric kindreds, which are neither descent lines nor descent groups." The usage I have adopted here, as most consistent with the way people on Yanuyanu talked about such matters, corresponds to the last mentioned.

[2] Sahlins's (1962) excellent and extensive ethnographic account of the kindred on Moala describes the aspect of Fijian kinship that I am referring to here as the *yavusa*. Sahlins uses the term *yavusa*, in that context, to mean the whole category of people with whom ego has kin relations rather than a specific collection of relatives with whom he or she habitually engages in actual enterprises. *Yavusa* was used in both ways on Yanuyanu, but I have adopted the latter usage, with the proviso that there are clearly core and peripheral members, and the situation determines how far the term is stretched.

Every person on Yanuyanu is at the center of a unique network of kin relationships; those relationships guide and give an essential dimension of meaning to his or her communication with others, and, at the same time, the relationships are created and embodied by such communication. Every communication event displays this dual, structural/practical, controlled/constituting impact simultaneously at the group and at the individual levels. Some communicative actions are more strongly associated with one level or the other, but in general I believe that most people are more aware of, and tend to think more in terms of, the individual, person-to-person dimension.

If one were to pick any person—man, woman, or child—on the island and follow his or her daily round of activities, one would find every interaction with others—and every action that could be construed as having an impact on such interactions—strongly influenced by one, or the combined effect of more than one, well-defined kin relationship. Such relationships do not by any means dictate every detail of the interaction, but they have a powerful shaping influence.

As Groves (1963) points out, the easiest way to understand the Fijian system of kinship terminology, which is of the general variety called a Dravidian two-section type, is to think of it as describing two intermarrying patrilines. A fundamental distinction, then, is between Us and Them—own patriline and other patriline (Figure 4.1). These are the two sections, and the assumed marriage rule is that a person of one section must marry someone from the other. Because the hypothetical sections are patrilineal, a man's children are assigned to his own section but a woman's are always members of the other section. This means that any person, male or female, distinguishes his or her father, the father's brothers and sisters, and the children of the father's brothers on the one hand—because they are "own" section to the person—and his or her mother, the mother's brothers and sisters, and the children of the mother's brothers, who are all "other" section.

In the person's pattern of discriminating among relatives by birth and marriage, generation makes a big difference. Two generations down, for example, all children are simply grandchildren, with no recognition of difference of any kind, and two generations up only sex is distinguished; as in English terminology, one can distinguish between male and female grandparents. At the generation level of minus one, the speaker distinguishes on the basis of section but not sex. Everybody of that generation is either an "own" child or an "other" child. With regard to marriage rules, they are all either children or children-in-law, whether actually or potentially.

In the immediately superior generation, plus one relative to the speaker, both sex and section are distinguished, as is rank based on

GENERATION	SECTION	SEX	TERM	EXAMPLES
own	own	own	*taci-*	male ego's brother female ego's sister
own	own	other	*gane-*	female ego's brother male ego's sister
own	other		*tavale-*	cross cousins
+ 1	own	male	*tama-*	ego's father, father's brothers, and so on
+ 1	own	fem	*vugo-* or *nei*	fathers' sisters
+ 1	other	male	*vugo-* or *momo*	mothers' brothers
+ 1	other	fem	*tina-*	ego's mother, mother's sisters, and so on
- 1	male ego's own, fem ego's other	both	*luve-*	male ego's or his brothers' children female ego's or her sisters' children
- 1	male ego's other, fem ego's own	both	*vugo-*	male ego's sisters' children, female ego's brothers' children
+ 2		male	*tubu-*	grandfather
+ 2		fem	*bu-*	grandmother
- 2			*makubu-*	grandchildren

Figure 4. I. Relationship Terms on Yanuyanu

order of birth. Thus there is a term for males of one's own section, which includes the father and the father's brothers, and the term can be modified to show that the brothers are either senior or junior to the father. All the women who are up one generation, own section, which would include the father's sisters, are given a specific term, and they can also be called "parent-in-law," given that hypothetically (or actually—the same term would apply in either case) they might be the parent of an other section man or woman that the speaker could marry.

Relatives of the other section in the superior generation would include not only one's mother but also her sisters, who could be characterized as senior or junior to the mother, and her brothers. The mother's brother can also be called by the term for parent-in-law, given that his children are possible spouses for the speaker.

Relatives in the speaker's own generation are also distinguished in terms of section, seniority within one's own section, and relative sex— that is, not male or female but own sex or opposite sex. Own section, own generation relatives include one's siblings—either own sex or other sex—and they can be distinguished as senior or junior to the speaker in rank. Parallel cousins, that is, the children of one's father's brothers, are included in the term for sibling.

Other section relatives in one's own generation, who would be the children of one's mother's brothers and one's father's sisters, are classified together under the terms for cross-cousin.

The kinship terms are not a perfect reflection of social reality, however. Actually there are far more than just two patrilines in the village. It would be quite possible, therefore to have an "own section" relationship with a person who is a member of another patrilineal social unit—another *mataqali*. One can also, given the ecclectic nature of *mataqali* formation, have "other section" relatives within one's own *mataqali*. The *mataqali* are not exogamous, and one can marry within them as long as the spouse is of the other section terminologically.

With regard to guiding interactions among individuals on the island—interactions that add up to the economics, politics, and so on, of the community—the relationship between the interactants is crucial. One behaves very differently toward, and expects different behaviors from, another person who is one's father, grandfather, cross-cousin, or father-in-law. But do people memorize long lists of possible moves and countermoves appropriate to every combination of relatives in every possible combination of circumstances? While many interactions may indeed be highly stereotyped and habitual in character, with the same circumstances and the same kinds of relatives involved again and again over the generations, the essence of the social process, like that of language, is that novel expressions are continually required. Fijian villagers, no less than people in urbanized, industrial societies, are perfectly capable of adapting their behavior to demographic, social, and technological change without having to abandon established relationship systems and invent totally new ones.

One almost always knows what to do in interactions, even novel ones, I would argue, because the relationship system governs behavior not by specifying scenarios in every detail but by controlling only the one most integral and dominating dimension: the character of communication possible between interactants. If the social process *is* communication, as I argue in this chapter, then rules of communication are the key element in the functioning of the social system.

In describing their own relationship system, my informants did not approach the topic from an overall, objective perspective as one outside the system might—giving an observer's account, as I have just done, of a "two-section system." Instead, they identified the key dyadic categories of relationship and specified how a pair with such a relationship should talk to each other. The important mutual relationship categories in everyday life are *veitamani*, the relationship between parent and child, *veitacini*, sibling to sibling, *veitavaleni*, cross-cousin to cross-cousin, and *veivugoni*, parent-in-law to child-in-law.

In each category, the rules of communication are very clearly defined, and I think they are best described in terms of two dimensions: freedom/restraint, and symmetry/asymmetry (Figure 4.2). Between pairs who are *veitamani* (parent–child) or *veitacini* (sibling–sibling), asymmetrical communication is expected, and in practical terms this pattern supports authority relationships within the hierarchically organized descent unit. Lines of command are clear because the parent or senior sibling is free to address orders and admonitions without restraint to the child or junior sibling. The child

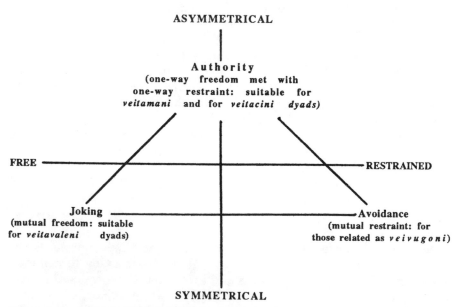

Figure 4.2. Patterns of Communication among Relatives on Yanuyanu Displayed on Axes of Symmetry and Freedom

or junior sibling enjoys much less freedom in addressing the senior relative, and this means no contradiction or backtalk. The *i tokatoka*, therefore, as an economic and political unit in the village can exploit its commonly held resources in an orderly and efficient way, with guidance from those with the most experience in farming, fishing, and so on. In community affairs, too, like the wedding described earlier, coordination of effort is assured, and this means that the social unit's actions project an effective, intelligible political voice in intergroup discourse.

When interacting pairs are *veitavaleni* (cross cousin–cross cousin) or *veivugoni* (parent-in-law to child-in-law), the pattern of communication is symmetrical in each case, but the two relationships are entirely different in character. Between a *veitavaleni* pair, for example, each is extremely free to address the other. The only thing forbidden to them, in fact, is something like scolding or commanding, which is asymmetrical in nature. Criticism or what would otherwise be harsh words are certainly possible between them, but what is said must be presented as joking, which can be answered in kind and which must not provoke a display of anger. The *veivugoni* pair's interactions must also be symmetrical, but they observe restricted communication toward one another. In fact, if at all possible they do not speak to one another directly but use third parties to route messages between themselves.

Relationships between individuals from different social units are generally governed by the rules of *veitavaleni* and *veivugoni* interactions. One's cross-cousins and parent-in-law are necessarily from another patriline, given the rules of exogamy, and most—though not necessarily all—other patrilines are in other *mataqali*. The "long arm" of the patriline, mentioned above in connection with the social group's ability to gather wealth and political support from far-flung sources, depends on lines of communication with outside groups.

Conceptualizing talk itself, or verbal performance, as an object of exchange gives some idea of the logic of the economic system that grows out of the relationship system (see Arno, 1976b). Between cross-cousins talk is unrestricted and therefore has virtually no "weight" in exchange, although it is essential in negotiating the terms of the exchange. Between cross-cousins, therefore, who lay claim to resources of different groups, exchanges are materially balanced. It is easy to request something from one's cross-cousin, and it is easy to refuse such a request. Words have such little exchange value between cross-cousins that one may freely take the property of another without even asking. This works both ways, however, so the other may retaliate and take back the object or its equivalent at any time.

Husband and wife are *veitavaleni* by definition—if they were not, they could not marry. They may speak freely to one another, and both are expected to contribute to the family economy. Appropriately, then, wedding rituals represent the relationship of equality writ large at the level of groups. Each feast, dance performance, whale's tooth, and ritual speech is answered tit for tat between the bride's and groom's side.

When speech is made scarce, however, it gains weight in exchange. A request from a person's *vugona*, for example, is made reluctantly and indirectly, but it is almost impossible to deny. Such requests are not made lightly or frequently, but they can be an important form of insurance when need is great.

In authority relationships, a request made to a father or senior sibling—or in the larger frame of reference to a chief—is not made lightly either, and it also carries great weight. A chief or a senior relative who is not able to give needed help loses his moral authority. Or, to put it another way, such failure undermines the social rationale for the deference paid to the chief in the form of restrictions on communication toward him. Likewise, a chief or a father does not depend on words to balance the flow of obedience and tribute paid to him. As we have seen, chiefs speak very little in ritual interactions. He or she largely remains silent while the chief's spokesman, the *matanivanua*, a representative of the land, makes the elaborate speeches appropriate to the occasion (see Arno, 1985b).

By definition the person in authority is not equal to the social inferior. It is not necessary, therefore, that the superior "pay" the inferior in the coin of valuable—restricted—speech. Exchanges between them need not be balanced in the flow of valued objects, material or verbal because social inequality is established by ideology and enforced by sanctions, whether physical or supernatural.[3]

TALK AS ACTION AND CONTROL

In this chapter and in the previous one, I have argued for a couple of equations. One is that politics, economics, and other major analytical dimensions of the social process on Yanuyanu island are identical with

---

[3] In contrast to exchanges between different *mataqali*, those taking place within a patriline represent a form of taking from one pocket and putting it into another. Balanced reciprocity is not necessary as nothing is really leaving the group. In the long run, junior members who must defer to their seniors today will be receiving such deference in the future, so the cycle is ultimately balanced. As noted above, cross-cousins are drawing from different corporate pockets, and exact balances is the rule in their exchanges.

the kinship system in its operation. This is essentially what most anthropologist have said about similar, small-scale societies. I have also argued that the kinship system in operation is in a real sense an exchange of messages. A presentation of food from one group to another is an action with inherent economic significance, but it might be a tribute from subordinate to superordinate, it might be an expression of chiefly largess in the other direction, or it might indicate the reciprocal support appropriate between equals. The meaning of the presentation, in other words, is an essential component of the social act. As structurally meaningful expressions—acts performed and interpreted in context of the communication system—such actions are messages and can be read in sequences of statements and responses.

The patterns of the sequences constitute the ground of social meaning in community life. A man or women returning from fishing might send some of the catch to his or her parents, parents-in-law, the chief, or to a visitor. He or she might also contribute some of the fish to the family cookpot. In each of these cases, a different structural message is uttered because in each the gesture is part of a different pattern constituted in abstract formal dimensions such as the symmetry, timing, direction of flow, and magnitude, as well as in substantive categories of shared ideology or meaning.

In describing the structure of the communication system as played out in concrete examples on the island, I have continually had to point to areas of disagreement and debate. One way to interpret this apparently high level of conflict is to define the social process, or culture, as struggle. Being participants in the same culture, then, does not mean being in agreement so much as being able to disagree—recognizing a particular pair of antitheses as not only debatable but worth debating.

I agree in part with this position, but I think it overemphasizes conflict—probably because conflict is highly salient and interesting to participant and observer alike. I agree with Malinowski's (1923) observation that the bulk of talk, not to mention all the other modes of communication in use in the group, reinforces and forwards the action taking place. Together with the communication system, which defines roles and governs the substance and the flow of messages among the role encumbents, such talk is indeed a mode of action.

But in his classic essay Malinowski argues that actors in primitive societies—defined as societies not initiated into writing and abstruse scholarship—do not engage in reflection, analysis, or criticism. What, then, are such people doing when they sit around the fire talking in the evening and are not engaged in fishing, farming, magic, or other recognized action? Drawing on his brilliant and influential conceptualization of language function as extending beyond the informational, Malinowski argues that the action they are carrying out is phatic communion, the reinforcement of existing social relationships through idle chat.

In the application of his theoretical insight to the analysis of life in primitive communities such as that of the Trobriand Islanders, the weight or credibility of Malinowski's example depends on an assumed contrast between primitive and civilized. In civilized society some people—scholars like Malinowksi and his readers—might use language to engage in pure intellectualizing that is essentially cut off from personal and social realities. The connection between that kind of talk and the business of making a living or enforcing authority is that of abstraction, so it is not part of the action it reflects upon. But in primitive societies, the argument runs, language is always tied to concrete action or to the maintenance of concrete social relationships.

Most people who read Malinowski's essay today, however, would object that its intellectual discussion of primitive and civilized societies was *not* cut off from the political and economic realities of the 1920s. It represented an indirect justification[4] for colonialism just as contemporary scholarly discourse is related to the justification of an emerging postcolonial world. It would seem that language—or rather communication—is a mode of action in both kinds of societies.

One way to characterize the use of language and other modes of communication in every society is to differentiate between two basic modes of action: communication that, embodying consensus, forwards the action of accepted practice and, in contrast, communication that constitutes a recognition, exploration, possible resolution, and in any case management of, the conflicts that arise in the process of social action.

In this chapter, and in the previous one, I have concentrated on the flow of structural communication that expresses or embodies in its patternings the relationships among individuals and groups that guide the political economy of the island as it takes concrete form. In describing it, however, I have alluded to many areas of contention and debate, and in the next chapter I focus on the specific configuration of the communication system that constitutes the second, functionally distinct form of discourse, which focuses on conflict. Among the many

---

[4] The term "justification" here needs to be used in a special sense. What I mean by it is not necessarily an explicit defense but performance of the real-making function of the network of cross-referencing and mutual support among the variety of discourse lines that make up community life. This idea will be discussed in the final chapter.

examples of overt conflict communication presented so far—and my observation is that in everyday life examples are abundant because almost any interaction can have aspects that are relevant to the more subtle, less explicit forms of conflict discourse—are the discussions among the members of Epi's group when they heard that they were to be excluded from a ritual (Chapter 3), and at a more formal level the island council meeting, briefly alluded to in that chapter, called to discuss Suka's right to cultivate at Baniu. The discussions at *yaqona* drinking sessions in which the *vanua* talked about *turaga*, and those at which the *turaga* talked about the *vanua* are also examples. At the national level of ethnic conflict or at the species level of gender conflict, even the *meke vakaidia*, the burlesque "Indian" dance, at the wedding, and the cross-dressing of the elder men can be seen as ritualized, group-level joking, and joking is an important element of communication about conflict on the island. Examples presented in the next chapter illustrate the pattern imposed by the communication system in the process of conflict management.

Preparing *Yaqona* in an Arbor During a Feast

5

Talk and Conflict: The Gossip System and the Kava Networks

Arrived there, the litle house they fill,
...
With faire discourse the evening so they pas:
For what olde man of pleasing wordes has store,
And well could file his tongue as smooth as glas:

Edmund Spenser, 1590,
The Faerie Quoone,
Book I, Canto XXXV

DISCUSSING, TELLING STORIES, DEBATING, AND JOKING ABOUT CONFLICT

Talking about conflict on Yanuyanu is an exquisitely complex activity, fully orchestrated by the rules of the communication system and allowing ample scope for embellishment by *virtuosi*. The structure of the process is provided not only by the rules for communication among kinsmen outlined in the previous chapter but also by a set of specific types of communication events (Arno, 1980, 1990).

Among these well-defined kinds of performances, some of the most important for conflict management in the village are joking, *veiwali*, debating, *veileti*, story telling, *veitalanoa*, and discussion, *veivosaki*, all of which take place exclusively among cross-cousins and remotely related relatives in other categories. Only people who enjoy free, symmetrical communication are able to engage without restraint in talk of this kind. Relatives who must observe restrictions avoid situations in which joking and the uninhibited exchange of views set the dominant tone of the activity. Such events might involve reference to taboo subjects such as sex or imply criticism of taboo relatives.

When kinsmen who are related as parent and child (*veitamani*), siblings (*veitacini*), or in-laws (*veivugoni*) are present together in a larger group, therefore, there is a general damper on joking and uninhibited discussion. In most cases one of the people so related— usually the junior of the two—leaves the group in order to relieve the generally felt awkwardness of the situation.

On Christmas night, 1971, I posed a question for discussion among the five men who had joined me to drink *yaqona* at the house I had been provided in the village. The question concerned the custom of "eating together," *kana vata*, during the Christmas/New Year holiday season on the island. Every year at this time the households within a descent group take all their meals in common, cooking jointly and eating under special arbors built for that purpose. I became interested in the practice because it offers an observable, behavioral expression of the kin group divisions in the community. According to my notes on topic, it appeared that more households that year than the last were not participating and had decided to eat as individual units.[1] My question to the group was whether or not this represented some kind of a trend away from the custom, and if so what the meaning was. As each person spoke in turn, the question came to be interpreted as why the "kinship way of life," *na bula vakaveiwekani*, was becoming weaker in Lau.

I was especially interested in the comments of Soko, who was a person I had not talked to much but who impressed me as perceptive and straightforward in expressing his views. An active, unpretentious man of early middle age, Soko lived with his wife, children, and an invalid elder brother in a well maintained compound on the outskirts of the village. He had extensive gardens and was reputed to be an

---

[1] That is, my notes reflected a high level of *talk* about nonparticipation. In fact, this turned out to be not much of an issue in the village after all. The year before, one household had refused to participate. Although there was much talk and speculation about the various people who might refuse this year, it turned out that everyone ended up participating.

Lauans living in Suva, the capital, speak with nostalgia about the custom of *kana vata*, which is more or less like a month-long family picnic. In the city people don't have the time, the space, or the food resources to carry out such an elaborate celebration, and they may also be separated from the relatives who would normally participate.

expert in the art of canoe building, although the absence of suitable timber on Yanuyanu prevented his practicing it. His father had been from Yanuyanu, but Soko grew up on Ogea island, where the family resided with his mother's kin, and it was there that he had learned canoe construction.

Finding their social position as outsiders a continuing burden and source of constant friction, he and one of his brothers eventually returned to live on their father's island. Here too, however, as one who had not grown up on Yanuyanu, he was a bit of an outsider, living in an isolated homestead far from the center of village activity. He was respected for his moderate ways, quiet good nature, and obvious competence in practical matters, but he was not a person many people knew well.

Although a number of people had come and gone during the afternoon and early evening, and the *yaqona* drinking had been continuous, only five men, aside from me, were present during the conversation reported here. One was Tui, my host, who was the owner of the house we drank in, and the others were Saqa, a friend from Korolailai who often came by to talk and tell stories, Vosalevu, an aggressively talkative, good-natured man, Waqa, one of Soko's brothers who still lived on Ogea and was visiting Yanuyanu, and Soko himself. Aside from the pair of brothers, everyone else was related to each of the others as cross cousins or very remote brothers or in-laws.

The first person to speak to the question about the decline of the kinship lifestyle was Vosalevu. He contended that the spread of enlightenment, *rarama*, was responsible. As people became enlightened, they realized that *kana vata*, in which a whole *yavusa* cooks and eats together in a continuous festival atmosphere for weeks on end around Christmas and the New Year, was too much work and was not worth the trouble.

Soko objected that this was a mistaken application of the concept of *rarama*. I might point out here that talk about *rarama* very often refers in large part to the coming and strengthening of Christianity, which serves as a synecdochal reference to Westernization and culture change, and Soko had been a staunch supporter of the church on Oqea.[2]

---

[2] The church is an example of an alternative communication system in the region. It does not seem surprising that a person in Soko's position, with less than optimal core kin links on the island, would seek out the church as a framework of roles and interaction that would allow greater scope of social activity and gratification. Being a *dauvunau*, lay preacher, is a position of authority within the church system, while being part of a family related to its largely patrilineal *i tokatoka* through a female link implies subordination.

Soko contributed a scenario that showed how the progressive abandonment of *kana vata* comes about. One year four men—for example himself, Vosalevu, Waqa, and Saqa—might agree to celebrate together. When the time came, Waqa might say that he could not contribute any money toward expenses for flour, sugar, and so on. Afterwards, the other three would gossip about, *kaseti*, Waqa, and he would become angry and refuse to participate the next year. The three remaining would agree to celebrate that year, but this time Saqa would fail to contribute. The others would gossip, Saqa would hear about it, get mad, refuse to participate, and so on.

Vosalevu then said that he agreed and that he was changing his answer: The reason for the weakening of kinship is *money*. Tui intervened to assert that Soko had been wrong to specify *rarama* as the cause. In true *rarama*, he argued, the four would get together and discuss the problem. They would decide that each man would put up ten dollars for the tea. In this way everyone was equal and some would not end up doing everything, as often happens today. Soko responded that he had specifically referred to a *mistaken* concept of *rarama*, and that in fact he also agreed with Vosalevu about money.

Waqa, Soko's brother who still resided on Ogea, kept quiet, and I asked him about *kana vata* on Ogea. In response, he asked the others to consider the meaning of the word "pound," *na paudi*. The others said yes, the old money (the English pound, formerly used in the colony). Waqa traced a circle on the mat with his finger and said that this meant the people were entrapped within a *lomanibai*, an enclosure or compound. In English this could have been expressed as saying that the people were impounded by the pound, and I assume his remarks were a translation of an English pun, which of course did not work in Fijian. But now, Waqa went on, is the time of *na dala kei na sedi*, dollars and cents. He opened his mouth wide, showing his teeth, and pointed inside. Now the pun was in Fijian, because Dala means both "dollar" and "open." The meaning of this, he said is "*sa kania na veiwekani na sedi*," "the cent eats kinship."

At this point everyone agreed that while money is the true source of the decay of kinship, no one can say why exactly. Tui said that before, he could ask Soko for a basket of *tavioka*, the staple root crop of the island, and Soko would give it to him. Or, he could just go to Soko's garden and pull it up without asking. But now Soko might want to sell his *tavioka*. "And," Tui said to Soko, "you know that I couldn't ask you for money or just take your money in the same way. That isn't a good thing to do, is it?"

Vosalevu said that earlier whole *mataqali*, or even whole villages, had *kana vata*. Then just *yavusa* started eating together. Now sometimes even smaller units are involved. The reason, he said, is that formerly the larger units were like families are now: Within a nuclear family, *matavuvale*, one does not count his contribution and weigh it against the others'.

Tui observed that in traditional life things do not have prices. For example, both *yaqona* and *tabua* (whale's teeth), the traditional items of the highest ritual significance, are not quantifiable—any amount or quality of either is sufficient for its purpose.[3] One *tabua* is the same as ten, and one ounce of *yaqona* is as good as a pound.

Tui went on to say that he had changed his mind about the question in any case. The true cause of the deterioration of kinship was overpopulation. Before, there were only a few people and there was plenty of copra for all who wanted to cut it. Two brothers would go together to cut copra to pay for the tea of their *yavusa*, and they would not think anything about it. Now, each has to guard his own trees because too many people use them.

Vosalevu agreed and said that in the old days one just cut copra and turned it in to the store—without money changing hands—and there was no disruption of kinship. It would be better, therefore, to have Chinese and Indians running the stores again and not have everyone handling money.

This led to a brief discussion of the issue of law and order. It was generally agreed that the police in Lau are ineffective because they are relatives of the people and cannot help being influenced by that. It would be better to have Indian policemen, the men argued. Tui said that the abolishment of the *Buli* form of government, which had established a separate government, in effect, for Fijian villagers in earlier colonial days, was a step backwards. Things are less orderly now, and people ignore communal work. He said this constitutes a retreat from *rarama* to *butobuto*, darkness.

As the conversation had now returned to its starting place with a reference to *rarama*, Soko chose to emphasize its church connotations.

---

[3] For example, a person who comes to drink *yaqona* with others brings some *yaqona* as his *sevusevu*, a mark of respect for the group. Even a very small amount constitutes the *sevusevu*, although as a practical matter a certain amount will be needed to keep the supply going during the evening. Consistent failure to contribute leaves a person open to joking criticism as a "mosquito," and it may be said ironically that "his smiling face is his *sevusevu*." Still, it is not proper to criticize the amount of the *sevusevu*. Also, any whale's tooth, regardless of its size, age, or beauty, creates the social obligation pertinent to the given ritual presentation. Large quantities of *yaqona* and *tabua* excite admiration and raise the general level of *marau*, happiness or pleasure, on both sides of the transaction, but quantity does not change the rights and duties created.

He said that even though the kinship lifestyle was weak now, it could be saved by the church. At this point Vosalevu, his cross-cousin interrupted to say: "Well, you claim that the church will strengthen kinship, but when you were a lay preacher on Ogea you raped one of your kinswomen (*ganemu*, "your sister"), so it didn't do much good then!" There was a tremendous outburst of loud laughter in the group, and for a long time no one could speak for laughing. Finally Tui said that Vosalevu was just too crazy. There was nothing he would not say. Soko laughed with everyone else, but he did not reply to the joking attack. When he finally rejoined the conversation, the topic had changed. Vosalevu had begun to criticize his cross cousin, Tione.

Tione was the storekeeper for the chiefly *mataqali*'s co-op, and Vosalevu said that he couldn't run the store properly because he was a drunkard. Tui told about Tione and some of his cronies having opened the store office at night to drink homebrew there. Eventually, as it grew late, the day's *yaqona* drinking drew to a close and everyone went home to bed.

That evening's conversation over the *yaqona* bowl was typical in the progression and mix of speech event types. The basic mode was one of *veivosaki*, a reasoned, free-flowing discussion of a serious topic. Because there was a defined topic, and it was one of somewhat academic interest in that there was no current conflict associated with it in the village, the pattern of talk verged on becoming a mild debate, *veiba*. Debating (see Arno, 1990) can be interpreted as a form of joking; it is essentially a form of verbal play and provides a chance to display one's wit and reasoning skills without being held to account for what one says. For example, it seems very unlikely that any of the men would really like to see the co-op stores returned to Chinese merchants or that they would approve replacing Lauan policemen with Fiji Indians.

Vosalevu's joking attack was a classic example in form, content, and timing. An effective joking remark strikes the victim suddenly and unexpectedly and yet has some logical connection to the flow of conversation. A joke is good—measured by the intensity of the laughter it evokes—to the extent that it would constitute a dangerous insult in any other frame or context of interpretation. Laughter seems to displace and disarm the potentially violent feelings and possibilities of physical retaliation that arise from serious accusations made in public. By laughing, the group clearly defines the remark as a joke and forbids its being taken as a serious attack.

The one thing about the conversation just cited that was extremely untypical was that Soko's true brother, Waqa, was present when the reference to Soko's sexual misconduct was made. This was a serious faux pas because although Vosalevu was related to both Soko and Waqa as cross-cousin and therefore could legitimately joke with either, one must never joke with one brother in front of another. Because of their taboo relationship, they cannot laugh about such matters together.

Furthermore, a person can be joked with about his or her own conduct only—never that of parents, siblings, or in-laws. It is thought to be unbearably shameful for a person to hear such talk about a taboo relative. If Tione's brother had entered the house while the others were criticizing Tione's homebrew drinking, for example, it would have been quite indecent for them to continue with that topic. I was told that skillful talkers can change topics instantly, without any telltale pause or unnatural changes in loudness or tempo, when someone who must not hear what is being talked about enters the house. On the other side, Lauans also consider themselves expert in detecting such polite deception. Unlike Europeans, one informant told me, "we Fijians can tell on entering a house that people have been gossiping about us [keitou, 'our group']. Our bodies know it. [Sa kila na yagonda]."

I think Waqa's presence, therefore, explains the unusual intensity of the laughter that followed Vosalevu's remark. The group had to override the extreme awkwardness of the situation. It also explains Tui's remark that Vosalevu was "crazy" and "would say anything." The circumstances made it impossible for Soko to respond to Vosalevu, and he simply remained silent. Normally a joking attack calls for an answer in kind.

The following evening, December 26, some of the same men again drank yaqona at Tui's house. Soko was there again, as were Tui and Saqa. Those who had not been there the night before were Mosesi and another pair of true brothers, Rusiate and Tepeli.[4] Soko's brother Waqa was absent this time.

The conversation came to be dominated by the veitalanoa, or storytelling mode from the first. There was none of the "academic debate" tone that had been instigated by my inquiries the night before.

---

[4] Although two pairs of brothers attended two nights in a row, my notes on who was present in the hundreds of yaqona drinking occasions I participated in over the year indicate that actual biological brothers rarely drink together, confirming informants' statements about the matter (see Arno, 1980). Both Waqa and Tepeli, Rusiate's brothers, were visiting Yanuyanu for the holidays and lived elsewhere. Tepeli lived in Suva, and Waqa on Ogea. They may have been curious about the American visitor and felt that drinking yaqona with me was harmless and a bit outside the bounds of usual social practice. Nevertheless, Rusiate and Tepeli did not engage in any joking, and no one joked with them during the evening in question. I never observed any other instance like Vosalevu's "crazy" behavior.

Still, it seems obvious in retrospect that there was a clear agenda, and the stories that were told were *vakabalebale*, with a point.

Mosesi told several stories about his experiences on Vanuabalavu, an island well to the north. One was about a *vesuvakaukauwa*, an attempted sexual assault, that involved a preacher and the wife of another church officer. The preacher ran away when the woman resisted, and afterwards he went into the bush and hid for several weeks. The men laughed, amused at the humiliation suffered by the hypocritical churchman, who represents somewhat of a stock character in village storylines—at least among those who are less than staunch in their support of the church.

After a slight pause, Mosesi went on to tell another story that he had heard. This one was about a man who was visiting a village that he was *tau vu* with. *Tau vu* is a social/political linkage, based on relationships among the origin spirits or gods of the traditional religion, between entire villages or regions, and the strongest kind of joking is permissible between their inhabitants. The men of the village knew that the visitor had achieved the rank of *talatala*, preacher, in his home village and decided to have him sacked for fornication. While a *meke* was being held elsewhere, they arranged for him to be alone with a woman cross-cousin of his. Once they were alone, the woman co-conspirator threw off her clothing and appeared completely naked before him—at which point he ran out of the house.

Everyone laughed at this story, and finally Soko took the opportunity to tell about the time he himself had been accused of rape on Ogea. He said he had been out fishing and was on his way back to the village when he met a woman who was hunting crabs. He joked with her and then went on to the village. He had forgotten about it until he started hearing that the woman had said that he tried to rape her. Soko said that he had been very surprised because it was completely untrue. The other men present said that it was regrettable, and they lamented the fact that people were only too willing to spread untrue gossip.

About a month later I accompanied Tui to one of his gardens, and he spotted Driva, a cross-cousin, approaching on the path. Tui shouted, "Here comes a man without *tavioka*. He is returning empty handed!" Driva laughed, and when he drew closer he said to Tui, "Just go right to Qeledamu!" and they both laughed. As we went on, Tui explained to me that Driva's remark had meant that Tui was to go to Driva's garden to get some food since he had none of his own. Tui said that most everyday joking among cross-cousins is about gardening—that is, failure and ineptitude in gardening. In a broader sense, he said, joking is about any bad thing a person has done that can't be talked about seriously.[5] If the reference isn't a joke, the person will get angry.

I asked Tui if he remembered Vosalevu's joke directed at Soko, and Tui said that was an example of what he meant. Soko could not have brought the matter up on his own, Tui explained, and Vosalevu's joke had allowed him to tell people the truth about what had happened. Otherwise people would have continued to gossip about, *kaseti*, Soko as they had been doing.

Although I myself had heard no one talking about or criticizing Soko, I could well believe that Tui was right about people doing so. Discussion and criticism of what people do is a constant activity in the village, and it is hard to imagine that anyone could escape it. A person who detects any questionable behavior loses no time in fashioning it into a *talanoa*, a story or anecdote, for the next *yaqona* drinking session.

One afternoon, drinking *yaqona* at a house in Korolevu, Matai said that he had solved the mystery of who had been stealing watermelons from the district school gardens. Walking to his own gardens earlier in the day with his young son, Mala, he had spotted a gang of small children hiding in the tall grass by the path. he investigated and found that they had some stolen melons with them. Matai called to Mala, who was playing near by, to come help him, and together they listed the names of the guilty children. At the mention of one name Tui said gleefully, "*Dauvunau!*" This referred to the fact that the father of the boy was a lay preacher in the church. I had heard people say on other occasions that this man had a habit of taking nuts from other people's trees to cut copra. The men present agreed that children such as the ones named had learned to steal because of their parents' example.

Matai said that in his opinion there was a lot of theft going on in the community, and another man suggested that there are those who actually live by theft. Someone else put in that Tione, the storekeeper, was an example of a person who lives by *kerekere*, asking favors from

---

[5] The connection between wrongdoing or failure and joking seems well accepted. Soko's elder brother, who lives with him in his outlying compound, is seldom seen in the village. I asked Tui about this once, and he said that the man does not like to visit the store, or other public area, when many people are likely to be around because he does not like them joking with him about his appearance. I had met him, and I knew that his face was severely disfigured. I asked Tui if he thought it proper for people to make fun of him for that, and Tui said it was because such things are the result of misdeeds; they are a supernatural punishment, just as gardening failure can be. It is proper, therefore, for his cross-cousins to confront him about it through joking.

relatives. "Everyday he comes to Bale and asks for tavioka," the man explained, "and Bale is getting tired of carrying it down for him."

"Well," Tui said, "this is why Sekope likes to drink *yaqona* with us—for the gossip!" Sekope, an older man who had just joined the group, protested that nothing could be further from the truth, that he detested gossip. This seemed to remind Matai of something, and he turned around to the group of small children who were playing in and around the door to the house as they listened to the adults talk.[6] He told them to *talanoataka*, "spread the story", to the other children the fact that the children he had named earlier were stealing the school's watermelons.

LECTURING, CRITICIZING, AND SCOLDING ABOUT CONFLICT

The pervasiveness of talk about others' conduct in the village makes it seem at times as though gossip is out of control and might represent a force destructive of order. In fact, "gossip", *kakase*, is strongly condemned by everyone in the community. Discussing and evaluating others' conduct, however, is not considered gossip. It is simply *veitalanoa, veivosaki*, and so on, and it is either appropriate or not depending upon the relationships among those present and those talked about.

It is only irresponsible talk about others—talking about things that one doesn't know for certain or at least have good reason to believe are true—that constitutes *kakase* for the villagers. One of the things that a person might be talked about and criticized for, in fact, is saying things recklessly and without regard for the truth. In this sense, the system of talk is self-policing.

Another way that accuracy is served is the open, widespread character of talk. The more people talk about factual issues, and the larger the groups in which they talk, the more sources of information will be tapped. The articulation of joking with storytelling, discus-

---

[6] Children on Yanuyanu seem to learn much more about the island's way of life by direct observation than by explicit instruction (see Borofsky, 1987). Not only informal ways of talking but also formalized rituals are absorbed in this way by children, who are not excluded from any public adult activities. Children generally surround and penetrate all such events, remaining quiet but watching and listening avidly. Notice, for example, the chapter-opening figure in which adults are clapping during an *i sevusevu*. Children of various ages are seen watching from the house in the background, and the little boy sitting close to his father on the left eyes on elder participant uncertainly and tries to imitate him.

sion, and debating also provides an important brake on groundless allegations. Through joking the person accused has the opportunity to present denials, arguments of extenuation, or alternate interpretations.

Looked at from the perspective of the communication system, however, the types of speech events and the channels of information flow discussed so far are only half of the story. As Figure 5.1 shows, a participant in the relationship system is part of a complex web that includes both symmetrical, free-flowing communication and hierarchical, restricted communication. Ego can engage in unrestricted communication with cross-cousins, and it is with them that he engages in discussion, debate, storytelling, and joking. With his or her *agnates*, however, Ego's communication possibilities are quite different. The speech events characteristic of relationships within the person's own patrilineal kin group include commands, reprimands, criticism, and scolding, each of which is a one-way, top-down form of communication.

This is not to say, of course, that everyday interactions within patrilineal groups and nuclear families are unpleasant or angry in tone. Just the opposite seems to be the case in general. When there is no conflict, the pattern of interaction flow is dignified and smooth, with virtually automatic displays of deference among the adults and older children. Very young children tend to be highly indulged and enjoy being the center of attention. They can be noisy, clamorous, and bold, and it is expected that they will violate all sorts of taboos and interaction rules because they are *yalo wai*, that is, their spirits or personalities, *yalo*, are unstructured, fragile, and immature, "as water", *wai*. As children grow older they seem to become very shy and quiet—almost stoic—inside the house, although they continue to be noisy, active, and demonstrative while playing in peer groups outside. In each situation their communication patterns—together with the shared conventional meanings attributed to those patterns—reflect, and largely constitute, their social positions.

Scolding, lecturing, reprimanding, and criticizing come into play within the patrilineal kin unit only in situations of conflict. And conflict, for present purposes, can be defined as a distortion or deformation of the accepted, structural patterns of communication that constitute normal social life. The patterns themselves, of course, are without inherent meaning or social significance. An injury—physical, economic, or psychic—raises questions of blame and redress only in relation to some rule, and rules evolve in social situations through shifting perceptions that one is or is not getting his or her due in social interactions. In conflict situations, then, one party or faction feels injured and perhaps outraged at the failure of the other party to perform in accordance with established expectations.

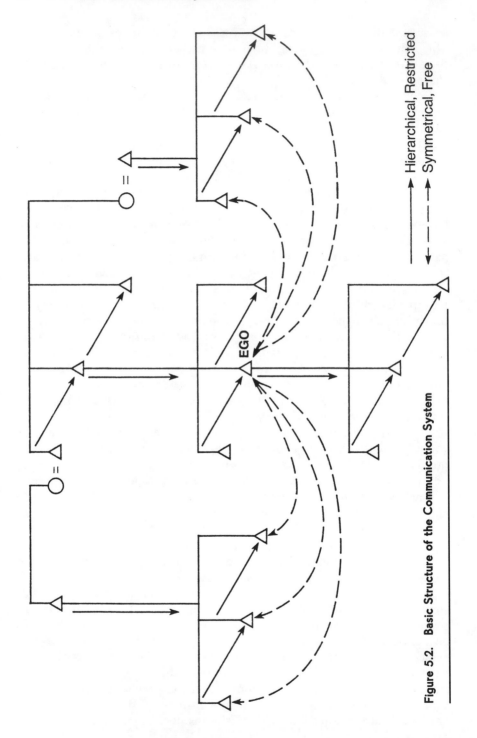

Hierarchical, Restricted
Symmetrical, Free

EGO

Figure 5.2.   Basic Structure of the Communication System

What happens next depends entirely upon the grammar of conflict behavior appropriate to the social situation. With regard to conflict within a Lauan lineage, the respective seniority of the persons involved makes every difference in the outcome. If the injured party is the junior, he or she is expected to do nothing and say nothing. This is the import of the stoicism of the elder child in a household. Children are not to voice complaints because it is up to the parents, and ultimately the parents' peers who may hear about and discuss the situation, to decide if the child's sense of violation is legitimate by group standards.

When Tui and his wife discussed giving away their 12-year-old son's pet horse, which Tui had given him to ride and take care of the year before, the boy's eyes filled with tears, and he bolted from the house, but he said nothing to either parent. Because the horse had been indirectly requested by his classificatory father-in-law from another island, who said he needed it because he had an operation and could not carry heavy things anymore, Tui felt he could not refuse (see Arno, 1976a). When I asked him about his son's reaction, he replied with some compassion that the boy was still *yalo wai*, immature, and would learn in time not to become so attached to things that he could not give them to relatives who needed them, which is the truly Fijian way of behaving.

The authority relationship created and sustained by the general pattern of communicative interaction between parent and child, *veitamani*, and elder and younger sibling, *veitacini*, is reflected in all aspects of intrakin unit activities. This one-way mode lends itself to instruction, correction, and punishment, and its functional logic in the process of social control seems clear when the senior is a well socialized adult and the junior a child who is still learning to conform to the group norms. But in the Lauan communication system, the pattern is enforced well beyond the arena of child rearing. Grown men and women are also subject to the authority of their elderly parents, and at times friction may result, given the particular circumstances and the personalities of the people involved. Strong-willed juniors might resist control, and equally strong-willed older people can hang on to the reins of power until the bitter end.[7] In most cases, however, it

---

[7] The transition of power between generations marks a perennial sore spot in Lauan social process. Along with the problems associated with the fissioning of groups that become too large, the relations between mature sons and their elderly fathers represent a structural source of conflict that is built into the process and must be dealt with by rituals of reconciliation (see Arno 1979a).

seems that elderly parents more or less gracefully relinquish decision making in practical affairs and enjoy a life of retirement, looked after by their children and providing their grandchildren with a ready source of solace, entertainment and instruction.

Epi, however, the leader of the junior branch of the chiefly family whose activities during the big wedding are described in Chapter 3, had not "retired" at all. A vigorous man in his seventies, he got up early most mornings and went to his gardens, several miles from the village, taking some cooked food with him for lunch. In the afternoon or evening he would reappear with heavy baskets of produce suspended from a pole over his shoulder. Arriving at his house, he would call sharply to his wife, a woman who although much younger than he did not appear to be nearly so active. She and their young, school-aged children would take care of food preparations while Epi bathed and dressed for a bit of *yaqona* drinking before dinner.

Epi's other children who resided on the island, two men and a woman, all middle-aged and fully engaged in rearing their own children and taking care of their own households, did not approve of their father's situation. When their mother had died, he had married her younger sister and started a new family, and this meant that his role as a provider had been extended. His younger sons were still not old enough to take over the gardening for the new household.

In conversations with his wife, Tui at times referred to his father's decision to marry again. They felt that his situation was unseemly and "pitiful," *vakaloloma*. "At his age he should be able to relax and drink *yaqona* with the other old men," Tui said. "But he has to go out and work hard every day."[8] Both Tui and his wife seemed concerned about the old man's health and comfort, but they were also critical of him and felt that it was his own fault. They indicated that he had demonstrated an overly strong will and had not shown proper concern for the peace of mind of his older children. Because of the authority relationships within their kin unit, however, there was virtually no one other than his wife to whom Tui could voice such sentiments, although his remarks indicated that his siblings felt the same way. Tui told me once that among his siblings only he and his sister truly loved their father, but they all regretted that their father had been so *lialia*, "silly." Certainly, mentioning such criticism directly to his father was out of the question.

One afternoon I was listening to Biau, a very old man who died later

----

[8] Epi himself had a different perspective. He told me that he loved to work hard because it kept him fit. He said if he ever missed a day working in his gardens he didn't feel well.

that year, tell about his life, especially his entrepreneurial activities as an interisland trader. Epi was there too, and Tui and his wife were in and out of the house while we talked. Biau explained that starting with a sailing canoe, he had worked his way up to owning a European style cargo boat as well as a concrete block store building on Yanuyanu before he went bankrupt. At one point he said that when his wife died he decided that, considering his advanced age, he would not remarry but would let his daughters and his son's wives take care of his cooking and household arrangements.

I don't remember how I responded, but I must have said, just being polite, that it sounded like a wise decision, because the next day, talking about Biau, Tui said to me, with a rather unusual intensity, "I was so glad to hear what you said to Ta ("Dad")!" I had no idea what he meant, and when I asked him he said, "You praised Biau for not remarrying right in front of him." Reflecting on what he said and the way he said it, I concluded that Tui intended in part to rebuke me for careless talk[9]—when speaking, one must be aware of everyone who is present and how they will interpret one's remarks—but that in part he did enjoy the mistake.

Without intending to, I became involved in another conflict between Tui and his father shortly afterward. Having explored the practice of *yaqona* drinking in the village for some time, I became curious about homebrew drinking, which was much talked about and seemed to have some social importance. In some ways it appeared to be the antithesis of *yaqona* drinking, being improper, nontraditional, and tending to result in disorder and uncontrolled conflict. I thought I should approach the matter with some caution because of the strong opposition to homebrew drinking by the local church establishment.

I mentioned my interest to several friends, and they said they would be glad to talk about it. Saqa, a mild mannered (*yalo malua*) young man from Korolailai, offered to provide a sample that we could taste as

---

[9] The longer I stayed on the island and the more I was presumed to know how to behave, the more I found myself being criticized. After many hours of sitting cross-legged in a *vale putu*, a house in which a multiday funeral observance was taking place, I said goodbye, stood up, and left. I was thinking how hungry I was and how much my knees hurt as I walked down the path outside. Suddenly Tui, having left right after me, appeared at my elbow and said with a bit of exasperation in his voice, "Good, Andrew! Just stand up and walk out." I thought I had done the proper thing by saying, using the usual phrase: "Well, I will go ahead now, please. You (all) will then follow later." But Tui told me it was rude to just stand up and walk out of a gathering like that. One must walk crouched over, with bent knees and torso twisted so that one hand leads in the direction of travel and the other trails behind the back. Instead of walking behind people's backs, as I had done, one has to go in front, saying "Tilou, tilou" all the way out. This demonstrates respect for the others.

we talked. He said he would brew some as soon as he could obtain the yeast, and asked whether I would prefer banana, tavioka, or pineapple. I discovered later that they all taste the same.

To avoid a situation that might lead to criticism, it was agreed that we would drink "in the European style," that is, the homebrew would be sipped from glasses or teacups, the drinking would take place in the afternoon so that participants could break off early and go directly home for dinner, and the supply would be limited to one teapot. Homebrew is measured in teapots and "balls," the large plastic or glass netfloats that wash ashore on the island at times and are drilled to make containers for liquids.

The drinking session took place at my house, which was normally Tui's, although he and his family had in large measure moved out to the nearby kitchen building, to allow me more room. While the rest of us drank, Tui himself abstained, explaining that he tended to drink too much and go crazy. The other men agreed that it was his major weakness and that drinking had been source of trouble for him for years—although not so much lately, as he had gotten older.

Tui said that the Roko, an important district government official who is selected from among men of high traditional rank, always used to stay in Tui's house when he visited the island. "One evening," Tui said, "the Roko told me: 'Well, Tui, you are not the only one. A lot of people are like pigs when they drink. They go naked and urinate in the street.'" Tui went on to say that when he was in Suva he never got drunk and caused trouble. Although European beer was delicious to him, he was determined not to waste money on it. He never bought beer, therefore, but he always accepted beers that were bought for him. He felt bad about this failure to reciprocate because it was *veivakaisini*, behavior appropriate to the lowest ranked sort of person in Fijian society, but that was his decision. If he drank in the village, however, he often went out of control. Because of his children, he said, he had more or less quit drinking beer. From time to time during my stay I had heard stories of how, in years past, Tui had gotten drunk and beat up people whom he felt deserved it. Although not a large man by Fijian standards, he was considered a fearless and highly skilled fistfighter, and his getting drunk and "going around the village" was viewed as a *ka rerevaki*, "a frightening event."

In the weeks that followed, several more groups of acquaintances dropped by with homebrew. When Tui was present he joined in, but he never drank to excess. One afternoon a small child, whom I recognized as one of Rusiate's, arrived with a note written in English on a small scrap of paper. It said: "Like a few cups beer? Please reply." I wrote: "O.K. Just a few," and gave it back to the little boy. Later, another boy appeared with a teapot of homebrew covered with a dishcloth. Presently Rusiate, a notorious homebrew drinker as well as an amusing conversationalist, appeared. He said that he had sent his son with the teapot because he did not want to be seen walking through the village with it. Several of our other friends would be along shortly, he said, as he had sent word to them.

By this time I had begun to have second thoughts about this method of investigating homebrew drinking. I feared it might be something that could get out of control, and I had been told already that there was gossip, *kakase*, about our drinking. I was somewhat relieved, then, when Epi came to the house one day when I was alone there and said, in a firm but not harsh way, "I am forbidding beer drinking in this house." He went on to say that he did not blame me and was not angry but that I should tell Tui and Rusiate not to bring beer there anymore. I said that that would be fine with me and that I did not really like homebrew anyway.

When I told Tui and Rusiate later that day, Tui's reaction was that Epi should have told him, not me. He said it was not Epi's or anyone else's place to *vakavulici*, "lecture or criticize," me, given that I was so highly educated, *vuku*. Also, he asserted, it was *his* house, and I could do anything I wanted there. Epi had been listening to the gossip of the old men and the *dauvunau* (lay preachers), who were themselves nothing but a bunch of thieves and reprobates, Tui said. Rusiate's response was a sly look as he commented, "Ah. He doesn't know about our batch of pineapple beer that is almost ready."

The next day Tui's wife told me that Sekope, an older man of the chiefly *mataqali* of Korolevu, had come by and asked for Tui's help in putting a new iron roof on an outbuilding in his compound. I dropped by there in the afternoon to see the work, and I found that the men had finished the job. Rusiate also showed up, and he insisted that Sekope celebrate the renovation with a beer drinking session. Everyone went home to bathe and dress, and we returned around 4 p.m. Rusiate brought the homebrew, and he acted as bar man, *ba mete*, spilling quit a bit, as he was already drunk, having started earlier. About eight men attended, and when the party broke up a few hours later, no one except Rusiate was drunk.

Tui and I ate dinner together, and his wife, Leba, brought the food in and served it. Presently Tui whispered to me that he was going out to look for more beer; he left, over the objections of Leba, who did not believe him when he said he was just going to the outhouse.

After typing notes for a while, I went to bed early but was awakened by the sound of Tui roaring up and down the village, bellowing like a bull. Feeling that on several accounts it would be best to keep out of the way, I went back to sleep, although I was awakened several times again by disturbances. At times I could hear Sekope and Kai talking, evidently trying to restrain Tui. At some point Epi entered my house and asked several boys who were sleeping in the outer room where I was.[10] When they said I was in the next room, sleeping, he addressed me and said that Tui was drunk. He asked me if Rusiate had given him the beer, and I said I did not know. All this was in total darkness. The village was absolutely quiet except for the occasional outburst from Tui.

Rusiate came by early the next morning to ask for a tin of beef from my supply. This was the sort of request I was very glad to accommodate in view of the quantities of fruits, vegetables, and fish that Rusiate and many others brought during my stay. He said that he had heard from one of his grandfathers about Tui's drunken rampage, and he said, in a conspiratorial sort of way, that it was a major blessing that the two of us had been asleep and therefore were not implicated in any way in the affair. He said that we should not drink with Tui any more because his drunkenness was too strong, and he was just like an animal when drunk. He said Tui would sleep for a long time because he would be too ashamed, *madua*, to face anybody this morning.

Tui's wife, Leba, and the children came over with a pot of tea and some biscuits, and as we ate breakfast they were full of talk about Tui's escapades during the night. Tione, the storekeeper, who was acting as wireless operator, came to the house on wireless business. He needed some change and a receipt, and it was Tui's job as wireless treasurer to handle such things. Leba wrote out the receipt, and she told Tione that Tui had spoken strongly to Takelo, the *matanivanua* of the island during the night. Tione said it was a good thing he had done so because Takelo deserved a talking to; he was not doing his job properly and was bringing the island to ruin.[11]

---

[10] Tui had given standing orders to the boys, two of his sons and one of their parallel cousins, who were around 10 or 12 years old, to sleep in the house. He explained to me that this would forestall gossip, otherwise inevitable, that I was meeting this or that unmarried girl there at night. The children did not like the arrangement much because I often stayed up late drinking *yaqona* with people who came by to talk, and this prevented their getting to sleep at a reasonable hour.

[11] The controversy over Takelo's performance in the post of *matanivanua*, "talking chief" or "herald," is an example of a particular conflict taking place along the fault line of the *turaga/vanua* relations in the scheme of traditional social organization. Tui was representing his whole chiefly *mataqali* in his attack on Takelo. They felt, according to many comments I recorded, that he was serving the interests of his own land *mataqali* and not that of the whole community. Specifically, he was accused of diverting *yaqona* presented in chiefly *sevusevu* to his own use and, by his own attitude and behavior, encouraging disrespect for the chiefly office.

When Tui finally got up at lunch time, the left side of his face was swollen badly. He said he must have run into a tree because he did not remember any fights. He said he had drunk too much and had become "excessively happy", *sa sivia na marau*. As the story of his activities gradually came out, it appeared that his specific "offenses" had been roughly four, aside from generally disturbing the peace of the village. He had entered a house where a group of unmarried young men had been drinking homebrew, taken over the allocation of drink in the group, and had engaged in several scuffles with them as they tried to eject him. Once thoroughly drunk, he had entered a house where Takelo and a group of mature men had been peacefully drinking *yaqona*, and he loudly harangued and verbally abused Takelo, frightening everyone. He went to his father's darkened house and stood on the house platform shouting that his father had no right to tell "Mr. Andrew" what to do. Epi did not answer him but told Korovou, who was standing nearby, to take Tui home and put him to bed. Tui then fell off the house platform, injuring the side of his face. Finally, Tui roused Kai, a parallel cousin, from his bed and dragged him to Marika's house, where he stood outside and challenged Marika to come out and fight. Kai was to act as a witness to the fairness of the fight, but Marika told Tui to go home and get some sleep, and Kai was able to persuade him to do that.

Tui told me that his having commandeered the youth's homebrew and his playful scuffles with them were nothing. They liked him, and they had all enjoyed themselves.[12] Also, as far as Tui was concerned, his lecturing Takelo was perfectly acceptable. He argued that discussions and *yaqona* drinking had been in progress in the house, and he

---

[12] Several days later I drank *yaqona* with Korovou, a cross-cousin of Tui's who had been present when Tui invaded the youths' drinking session, and he gave the following account as a humorous *talanoa*: Tui barged uninvited into the house demanded to drink beer belonging to three young men. Korovou warned the youths not to give Tui any beer, but soon Tui was controlling the drinking, deciding when rounds were to be served.

They started to fight over it, the boys against Tu, inside the house. Korovou merely watched and drank the beer, as it was obvious that they were all equally drunk. (There seems to be an accepted idea that unfairness in fights results from unequal drunkenness.) Then they all went outside and fought in the open for a while. Korovou took the opportunity to leave and take the beer with him. He was afraid that in the commotion the beer would be spilled and wasted.

The boys came back, and when they discovered the beer was missing they went out to look for it. Korovou then reentered the house and drank beer by himself. Presently they all came back with Tui. As if nothing had happened, they sat down and said *Taki!*", "Pour!" After a while they started to give each other sidewise glances—Tui and the boys on either side. Then they began to glare at one another. (Korovou acted out this part of the story.) And then they started up the fight again.

had merely added to the debate with some serious comments about Takelo's performance of community duties.

His challenging Marika and defying his father, however, were serious problems that he would have to deal with immediately by way of ritual apology, *i soro*. Because they were matters "within the yavusa," the *i soro* could be informal in character (Arno, 1976b), and that evening Tui called for Kai and they went to Marika's house where he was eating dinner. Tui tossed him a small bundle of *yaqona* and said that it was because of what he had done. Marika said it was nothing serious and that he had already forgotten about it.

Taking *yaqona* to apologize to his father, however, was something that Tui agonized over for several days. He had the *yaqona* ready, but he couldn't face the necessary apology. He said he was ashamed for not following his father's words, and also he didn't want people to see him going through the village carrying *yaqona* to his father. He said his father would stay away until "we" brought *yaqona* or until his anger cooled off. (I was somewhat taken aback at his use of the dual inclusive "we," *daru*, including me as a party in his *i soro*.)

Tui volunteered the idea that he had gone out and gotten drunk in order to defy, *bolea*, his father. Reflectively, Tui observed that when he and his brothers were growing up their father had disciplined them and spoken harshly to them almost every day for small transgressions. He was a *qase yalo kaukauwa*, a harsh-spirited old man, Tui said, and he was wrong to act that way. Unfortunately, he said, this treatment "taught me," *vulici au*, to be the same. This is why today he can't stand to be restricted in anything he does. This is why he used to get drunk and give away all his clothes, except his underwear; which is why the former Roko had told him, in a mock comforting way, that others were like pigs too when they drank. Tui said that he tries not to be harsh with his own children and not to whip them—he doesn't want to be like his father in this respect—but sometimes he does anyway, which is pitiful for them.

After several days Epi came to the house early in the morning, before breakfast. Tui, Leba, their children, and I were sitting around talking when he entered. He went directly to the upper end of the house and sat in a chair;[13] without waiting for a strained atmosphere to

---

[13] This was very unusual. Normally even high-status persons would not sit in a chair when others are sitting on the floor. In one sense, his action emphasized his authority and his right to criticize us in that he put himself in an elevated position; at the same time sitting in a chair is a very nontraditional, "modern" thing to do, and this aspect may have taken the edge off the situation a bit, softening the impact and lending an air of informality. Epi's choice of clothing was consistent with this aspect of the message; he was dressed in his work clothes and was on his way to his gardens.

develop, he launched directly into a lecture about the evils of drunkenness. Becoming more specific, he again said that he was not angry at me but blamed only Tui and Rusiate. He said he did not want to see Rusiate's face around there again and added that Rusiate's wife had left him and had gone back to her own island for several months, earlier in the year, because of his drinking.

Tui said, in a somewhat subdued, embarrassed way that we were preparing to bring him some *yaqona*, and he threw the small bundle on the floor near Epi's feet, much as he had done when he had apologized to Marika. Epi picked up the *yaqona* and formalized the situation somewhat by giving a short acceptance speech ending with ritual clapping and verbal formulae, in which everyone joined.

TALK AS A CONFLICT MANAGEMENT SYSTEM

The illustrations discussed so far in this chapter, in which villagers have talked about conflicts either in the open, joking way associated with cross-cousins and remote relations of other kinds or in the anxiety-charged, one-way channels within the patriline, represent aspects of the conflict management mode of the communication system that an individual would encounter in the daily round of village talk. In other words, the process is dispersed, fragmented, and distributed in time, space, and personnel. There is no specific forum where one can go to hear the case of the stolen watermelons, the rape of the crab hunter, or Tui's disturbance of the village peace being presented, debated, and resolved. Instead, virtually every social occasion involves disconnected parts of one or more conflict cases at various stages of their management. Most new instances of conflict involve the revival of earlier ones, and in fact none of them, unless the extremely trivial, is ever resolved in the sense of being over and forgotten.

Villagers, as participants in the dominant, traditional, kinship-based communication system, engage in conflict management automatically, as it were, without being particularly aware of the process as process. People play their assigned parts without reflection on the institution, which becomes visible to analysis only from the perspective of the overall communication system.

Figure 5.3 is a model of the conflict management configuration of the communication system, and it portrays the functions of the social process. Male and female systems are similar but largely separate and parallel in operation, and I present here the male version. Ego represents a person who comes to be identified as a wrongdoer. For any Ego, there are a specific set of others who are related to him in such a

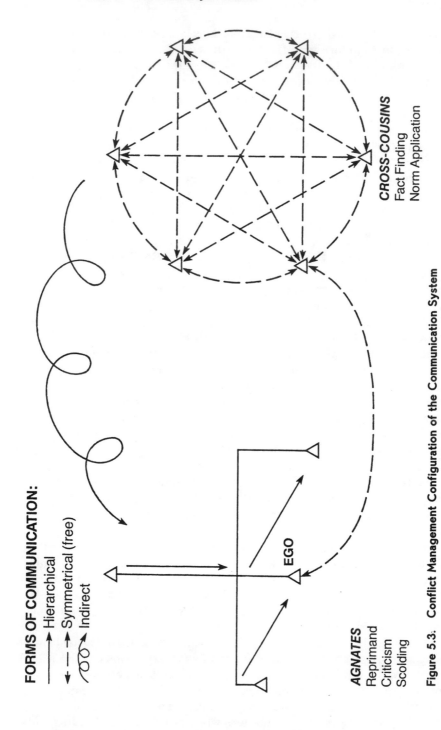

FORMS OF COMMUNICATION:

→ Hierarchical

←--→ Symmetrical (free)

〜〜→ Indirect

CROSS-COUSINS
Fact Finding
Norm Application

AGNATES
Reprimand
Criticism
Scolding

EGO

Figure 5.3.   Conflict Management Configuration of the Communication System

way that they are free to, and in fact are highly motivated to, discuss and evaluate his behavior in minute detail and with full consideration of his personal and family history. Ego may join in—or be forced in—through joking, and he can present his side of the story.

Meanwhile another set of people, specifically defined by their relationships to Ego, are not enjoying the situation at all. The members of Ego's patriline are "protected" from the talk that is going around the village because of the intense shame, *madua*, they are expected to feel. Actually their exclusion from the talk probably produces or intensifies negative feelings that are culturally labeled as *madua*.

Shame, along with the associated processes of social identification and rivalry, *veigati*, that motivate the participants' eagerness in examining and evaluating others' behavior, forms the psychological engine that drives the conflict management discourse. *Madua* itself, as well as the total conflict management institution, can be defined in communication terms. It represents a situational, temporary raising of the threshold of communicative freedom.

For example, when an individual in a social situation is exposed to a shame-producing event, he or she "*sa cuva*," ducks the head and crouches low, looking straight downward and remaining silent. This stereotyped behavior instantly cuts off visual and verbal contact with the others present, who may try to repair the situation. If an adolescent brother and sister, for example, are present when someone—through mistake or reckless disregard of propriety—makes a sexual joke, they are stricken by shame, unable to talk or look at the others, and the rest of the group quickly change the topic until one of them has a chance to withdraw. In the course of a case that I observed in the village, a man was present in the wireless shack when a message addressed to the police was read reporting that his classificatory sister had been sexually assaulted (see Arno, 1980). His reaction was to *cuva*, and later people talked about how the situation should have been avoided by some artifice that would have caused him to leave before the message had to be read.

The relationship of *veimaduataki*, mutual shame, arises between any relatives who are engaged in an active conflict. It is expressed by avoidance and experienced as a sense of awkwardness in one another's presence. If the relationship is a free one to begin with, as between *veitavaleni*, cross-cousins, a note of restraint is introduced, while relationships of restraint like *veitamani*, parent and child, see intensified avoidance. Ritual resolution by *i soro*, or in some cases just the passage of time, allows the level of freedom and restraint to return to normal.

Referring again to Ego's patrilineal relatives in Figure 5.3, one can see that shame, as a structural phenomenon—a functional deformation of the communication patterns that they are part of—is thrust upon them, whether or not they would have spontaneously "felt" it as an emotion. To repair the situation, those who are senior to Ego must correct his behavior through criticism, lecturing, and scolding. If the conflict is between younger men from different *mataqali*, the elders of either kin unit may also intervene directly and initiate an *i soro* from one group to the other, taking the matter out of the hands of the individuals who started it. This kind of action is a clear expression of the accepted idea that a person's actions are attributable to his group, and that therefore there are no strictly interpersonal conflicts.

An individual engaged in conflict with another may take a number of actions that may be read as elements of informal conflict management procedure (Arno, 1979b). The most common I observed or heard about were violent self-help or retaliation, an appeal to public opinion through talk, avoidance of the other party, appeal to authorities, reporting the other to the police, and use of the ritual apology, *i soro*.

Generally speaking, violence tends to take place early in the dispute, and avoidance may begin early also and continue until there is some kind of resolution. Resort to the police is seen as punitive, and it usually is employed only after the injured party has garnered support for his action through talking to his cross-cousins in *yaqona* drinking contexts. Appeals to traditional or quasitraditional authorities—either local or national—demonstrate respect for hierarchy, the key concept of the system, while prolonging the state of conflict. Only the *i soro* is finally capable of establishing normal relations.[14]

But whatever actions may be taken in the course of a conflict, the conflict management system through talk is constantly engaged and exerts a major influence on the outcome. For this reason, any inves-

---

[14] The *i soro* is not absolutely final, of course. I have argued elsewhere (Arno, 1979a) that it does not reach the practical, rational dimensions of the injury, nor does it deal with the underlying structural causes of conflict that derive from the relationships of social inequality and competition that are inherent in the Fijian system of social organization. By appealing to deeply held common values, the *i soro* is able to transcend everyday conflicts and provide a basis for continued interaction in the normal mode.

For example, when Tui challenged Marika to fight, it was because of Marika's having injured him in an "unfair" fistfight several years earlier (see Arno, 1976b). Marika had performed the *i soro* to Tui, and the two had been able to interact normally afterward, but at a certain level Tui was still angry. He had to be drunk, however, and therefore outside the bounds of normal behavior, to reopen the matter—just as he had to be drunk to openly criticize his father. Once sober, he used the *i soro* to repair his relationships with both other men.

tigation of conflict management and the indigenous legal process must attempt to clarify the workings of talk. As an institutionalized functional response to the need for social control, it arises at the interface between the social and the physical worlds and is reflected in the communication system.

THE KAVA NETWORKS

In the accounts of my investigation of the communication system on Yanuyanu presented so far, I have relied upon specific examples of talk and regarded them as case fragments that have largely confirmed the general statements about the rules of talk provided by in-depth interviews and conversations. Figure 5.3 represents a model that outlines the structure of conflict talk, and by structure I mean the regularities in practice that derive from the character of the institution and not directly from the conscious intention of participants as they enact that institution.

Once a model of institutional structure is proposed, it can be investigated at a variety of levels both to explore the empirical instantiation of the institution and also to learn more about its operational details. In the present case, examining conflict management on Yanuyanu, I wanted to look not only at the details of specific conflict incidents but also at the overall pattern of operation, independent of the particular case.

The empirical structure of the hierarchical part of the model of communication flow can be investigated in a straightforward way through the collection of genealogies. In genealogies—given the rules of communication already established—one sees laid out the actual authority structure of the community. The relationships they define are, for the given individual, relatively few and generally of great importance in everyday life.

Nonhierarchical communication, on the other hand, presents a more difficult problem for empirical investigation. Each individual has a great many cross-cousins and remote own-section relatives with whom he or she might interact, but not all of them play equally important roles in conflict matters. What is needed is a way to go from the statement of potential symmetrical conflict communication, as defined by genealogical data, to an account of the actual pattern.

One of the obvious questions that arises in this kind of analysis is that of just how numerous relatives in the various categories are likely to be, on the average. To get a rough idea, I asked four men, heads of households from different *mataqali*, to say how they were related to each man in a list of the 85 other heads of household on the island. The average response was that about 30 relationships were *veitavaleni* (cross-cousins), 20 *veitacini* (siblings), 20 *veivugoni* (father-in-law/son-in-law), 10 *veitamani* (father/son), 4 unknown, and 1 *veitubuni* (grandparent/grandchild). As Sahlins (1962, p. 164), points out, questions like these reveal preferences for relationships as much as facts of biology and marriage, given that alternate kinpaths may allow a person to consider a particular relative either a cross-cousin or a parallel cousin, for example. Also, because of the kind of people I asked and asked about—all married male heads of household—certain relationships could not appear. For example, children and elderly dependent members of households were not asked about, and neither were women.

My reason for selecting these limits was to map out what seemed to be a more or less bounded "conflict community" whose members would be expected to deal with conflicts among their ranks. To get a more full picture of village life, it would be quite essential to investigate conflict talk among women as well as men. I was not in a position to do that, although comments from women informants indicated that the women's system of conflict talk on Yanuyanu is similar to that of men but largely separate. Female cross-cousins joke with one another about, and evaluate, one another's behavior, and senior siblings criticize and correct their juniors.

On another level, it might be that children of a given age group form a semiautonomous conflict community, as Matai's comment indicated when he told the children to "talk about" the melon stealers among themselves. Certainly the *cauravou*, the unmarried male youth of the island, drink *yaqona* frequently among themselves, almost never joining the mature married men; presumably they talk about topics, including conflicts, of particular interest to themselves. A larger study that included a number of the conflict talk circuits on the island and traced the linkage among them would be of great interest, but for purely practical reasons of time and access to natural conversations, the present report is limited to the conflict talk among mature married men.

One important linkage between the male and female conflict talk circuits on the island did appear from my interviews, however. The connection labeled "indirect communication" between the hierarchical and symmetrical parts of Figure 5.2 is largely implemented through married women. Because of the structural ambiguity of her position, a married woman has privileged access to the communication flows within two patrilines—her own and her husband's. For example, Ego in Figure 5.3 may commit some offenses that has set the village talking—exposing not only Ego but Ego's whole patriline to criticism.

Ego's elder brothers are shielded from the talk, and theoretically they should not know exactly what sort of things are being said. On the other hand the elder brothers' wives, being cross-cousins of Ego themselves, can easily participate in the talk and learn what others outside the patriline are saying. It is quite appropriate for wives to tell their husbands in private, with perfect frankness, what is going on.

A woman is as concerned with the reputation of her marriage kin group as are her husband and children, but the rules of the communication system allow outsiders to speak freely about that group in front of her. Similarly, her husband can tell her what people are saying about her own patriline members—her brothers and sisters, for example— and she is in a position to rebuke those who are junior to her.

A salient feature of the communication system of the island community is the barrier to the flow of talk between men and women. While men say they can talk more easily with their mothers than with their fathers, and daughters experience slightly more freedom in talking with their fathers than do sons, talking freely with one's actual or potential in-laws of the opposite sex is discouraged for both men and women. And within a person's own generation the barrier is also strong; unmarried cross-cousins of opposite sex communicate in ritualized, highly public joking performances, such as called out sexual innuendoes and raucus laughter in groups. Serious, intimate conversation is appropriate between cross-cousins married to each other, but otherwise would imply something scandalous—the degree depending upon the marital statuses of the participants—and might provoke censorious comment in the village. Brothers and sisters practice mutual avoidance and rarely speak casually to one another.[15]

Given the nature of the communication system, therefore, talk about village-wide conflict cases takes place in two major, interlinked circuits, male and female. Opportunities for carrying out conflict talk, which is structured in each case by the relationships of the people involved, depends on the availability of settings in which the appropriate forms of communication are possible. Women visit one another in their houses and kitchens, and they also form into work groups, based on affinity and kinship, to carry out tasks related to fishing, barkcloth

---

[15] This does not imply that the bond between them is weak, however. On the contrary, it indicates deep mutual respect, and brothers and sisters are concerned about one another's welfare. In terms of the argument presented in the previous chapter (and see Arno, 1976a) that restricted—scarce—speech has enhanced value in the economy of discourse, a sister's request for material objects is weighty, and this is consistent with the *vasu* institution through which her children have a powerful claim on her brother's property.

production, and preparations for ritual exchanges. Women virtually never engage in *yaqona* drinking.

Among men, however, informal *yaqona* drinking is an everyday event that provides ample scope for conflict talk. It occurred to me, therefore, that networks among male *yaqona* drinkers would provide a representation of the institutional structure of the symmetrical part of process just as patrilineal genealogies provide a representation of the hierarchical. Accordingly, I asked every resident married man on the island to name the people he generally drank *yaqona* with.

I was able to talk to 80 men, and each named from zero to twelve of the others as people with whom he generally drank. Most people chose from two to six others, and in turn they were chosen by a slightly smaller number than they chose. Some did not name any drinking partners—explaining that they did not drink *yaqona*—but were chosen by others. On the other hand, some chose others but were not chosen by anybody. There were a few who did not choose anyone else and were not themselves chosen by anybody. Three men were chosen by a strikingly large number of others. Tione and Semiti was chosen by 18 each, and Motu was chosen by 31 of his fellows.

All together, there were 352 choices, and only 86 of those were reciprocal. That is, there were 43 instances in which A chose B and B also chose A. In no case did the person being questioned know the choices that others had made. I was surprised by the nonreciprocal nature of the choices, and in order to explore the finding I compared the two persons in each choice pair in terms of age and descent group. In the 43 cases of reciprocal choice, the drinking participants tended to be about the same age—in 20 instances they were from 0 to 5 years apart, in 9 cases from 6 to 9 years, in 7 from 10 to 14, and 6 from 15 to 18. In one case 51 years separated the two men. Thirty-one of the reciprocal choices were between men of different *mataqali*, while twelve were intramataqali.

The nonreciprocal choices, of which there were 266, offer the opportunity to examine directionality in the choices. I thought it might be possible that people tended to choose either up or down in terms of age or, given the hierarchical ranking of kin groups, descent, and that would explain why the choices were not reciprocated. In fact, the data show no such tendency in either dimension. In the area of age differences, for example, 10 choices linked people of exactly the same age. While 46 indicated people 1 to 5 years younger than the chooser, 50 choices were directed to those 1 to 5 years older. Similarly, 30 choices indicated people 6 to 10 years older, and 31 choices indicated people 6 to 10 years younger than the chooser. At 11 to 15 years, the distribution of choices was 22 up and 27 down, while at 16 to 20 years difference the figures were 12 and 15 respectively. At 21 to 25, three choices were up and six down, and so on. A similar but not quite so strikingly symmetrical distribution characterized choices between higher- and lower-ranking descent groups.

My interpretation of the nonreciprocal nature of the choices is that *yaqona* drinking is not a matter of cliques that are exclusive in character. Clique formations, I think, would tend to exacerbate conflict and restrict the flow of information and the variety of opinion expressed. Instead, consistent with the picture of conflict management communication I formed from my interviews and scattered participant observations, *yaqona* drinking is quite free, and choices respond to the nature of the particular topic of discussion, which varies widely and frequently in the conflict community. While a man might easily name a handful of people he drinks with, the topic-sensitive character of the pattern of talk means that he might as easily have named others in the circuit. Those chosen could well in turn miss naming the ones who named them.

My model of conflict management by talk in the village also predicts that people will choose to drink *yaqona* with cross-cousins and not with relatives with whom they must observe restraint in communication. Aside from a relatively small core of close kinsmen, however, links of blood and marriage can be remote and ambiguous, with several ways of reckoning being possible. When I asked each man for his choices, I also asked what relationship he had with each person chosen. In most cases in which some relative other than a cross-cousin was designated, the relationship was so remote that the two would not have to observe restraint. For example, while there were 94 choices in which the drinking partner was designated as a "brother," in 72 instances there was no genealogical link on the patrilineal side, and the two persons were not members of the same descent group. Of the others, five were members of the same *mataqali* but did not know of any patrilineal link between themselves. Four of the remainder had their father's father's father's father as the closest link, five of father's father's father, and six the father's father. Of the 94, only two were sons of the same father, and in neither case was the choice reciprocated.

The results of the survey show, then, that some people consider themselves more active in drinking than others, and some people are considered more attractive drinking partners than others. It is also evident that people choose to drink with cross-cousins or others with whom they have easy relationships, characterized by freedom in communication, and they avoid drinking with close patrilineal kinsmen. The picture that emerges from an examination of *yaqona* drinking partner choices thus tends to confirm an important feature of the model obtained through qualitative means. What remains to be demonstrated, however, is the linkage between the coordinate communication that takes place at *yaqona* drinking sessions and the hierarchical communication characteristics of the lines of authority within patrilines.

In order to examine this connection through my survey data, I compared the drinking choices given by persons who were linked genealogically as brothers. What I found in my samples of this material was that there is almost invariably some connection between the kava drinking partners of a set of brothers. I should point out again, however, that the choices do not represent firm cliques, and the results of this analysis should be weighed accordingly. Still, the choices do represent some kind of weak preferences. As Freud argued, even free associations, and the order of such associations, are firm facts, and they do mean something.

Four common patterns of linkage emerged from the data: in the first type, each of the brothers chose another person, who did not choose either of them in return; the second pattern involves a reciprocated choice between one brother and another person, who is also chosen by the other brother; the third pattern resembles the second except that the person who has the reciprocated choice with one brother chooses the other brother, who does not choose him; the fourth pattern is observed when one brother chooses another person who then chooses the other brother. In each of these instances, a third party represents a link between brothers and closes a communication loop that incorporates both hierarchical and symmetrical styles.

The nature of that link, however, must be conceptualized in light of the specific rules of conflict talk in force in the community. If A is the elder brother of B who engages in some kind of unacceptable behavior, C does not represent the kind of indirect link through which the two brothers can know each other's actions and views. On the contrary, C is specifically prohibited by rules of etiquette and common decency from mentioning to A anything he knows or has heard about B's misconduct.

Indirectly, perhaps through his spouse, A does know that his usual drinking companions are talking about and criticizing B—and by extension the whole patriline, including A himself—but he knows they must conceal it from him face-to-face. The effect, I believe is to make A uncomfortable in his relationships with his normal drinking companions. If B, the miscreant brother, has his own exclusive set of friends who discuss and evaluate his behavior, A need not be much concerned because he is isolated from the matter. If he never interacts with B's friends, he may care little what they think or what they are saying. When A's drinking friends coincide with B's, however, social pressure is brought to bear on A in a subtle but effective way. This, I believe is the significance of the third party I have labeled C. And C represents not only himself but also the group of people with whom he normally drinks.

Figures 5.4, 5.5, and 5.6 provide an example of the kinds of linkages that emerge from the network analysis. Figure 5.4 shows the male heads of household of an *i tokatoka* within the land *mataqali* of Korolevu, and it indicates their patrilineal relationships to one another as well as the *yaqona* drinking choices each gave. Figure 5.5 indicates the linkage among the brothers of the *i tokatoka* through their choices, which fall into patterns I, III, and IV.

As I mentioned above, these linking drinkers should be considered not as end points in information flow but as conduits—one should consider whom *they* talk to as well. Figure 5.6 shows the drinking choices made by the men who link the *i tokatoka* members. Immediately one is struck by the emergence of Motu as a second-order linker in the talk system. Motu was one of the men who received far more choices, 31, than the average. I looked at the drinking choices of ten other sets of brothers, and I found that Motu figured in the connections between nine of the sets.

This information, which I discovered only after I had left the field, raises several questions. Who is Motu, and what is his role in the structure of conflict management on the island? I must admit that his role was not at all evident to me during my stay in the village. Looking through my notes, searching for references to him and records of his contributions to conversations, I conclude that Motu was well-liked and active in *yaqona* drinking. He seemed a quiet, modest, sensible man, not particularly noted for his wit or unusual storytelling skills. He was not a person of high rank or ceremonial position within the community, and in fact the opposite might be said to be true; he was one of those, like Vesu and his brothers, whose fathers had changed *mataqali*, and there was some talk about the insecurity of his position. Although he was frequently referred to as someone who loved to drink *yaqona* and talk, I never heard him described as a gossip, *tamata dau kakase*.[16]

---

[16] One of the things I tried to keep records of during my fieldwork was any reference that came up in natural conversation in which another person was evaluated in some way, positively or negatively. The only "case"—that is, in my usage, a connected series of communication events focused on an instance of conflict—in which Motu figured was one in which it was said that he was careless in burning in his gardens and started a fairly major grass fire. This was talked about as a violation of a government ordinance covering village affairs and could have resulted in a fine if reported and pursued. No "action" was taken, in that vein, but the transgression was duly noted and permanently engraved in the village memory through talk.

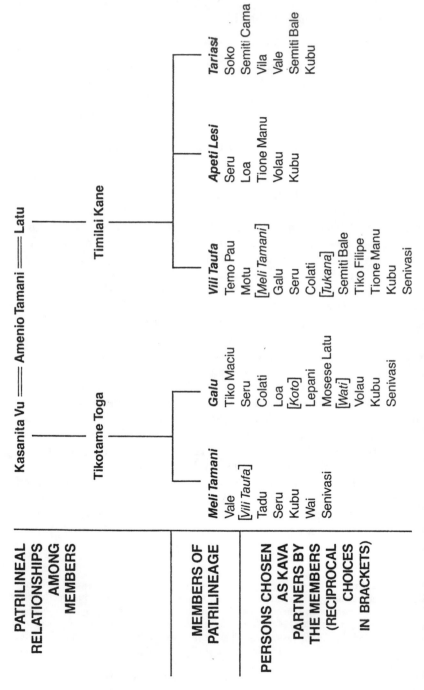

Figure 5.4.   Members of a Patriline and Their Choices in Yaqona Drinking

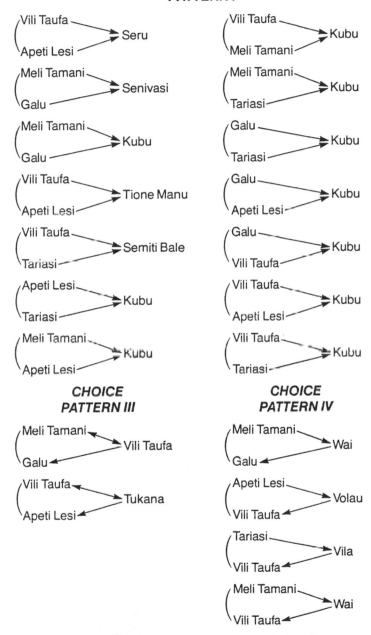

Figure 5.5.   Patterns of Linkage among the I Tokatoka Members

Kubu
Motu
Tukana
Lutu
Lepani

Tukana
Semiti Cama
Motu
Vili Taufa
Apeti Lesi
Semiti Bale
Dua

Tione Manu
Motu
Biu
Waga Filimone
Ledua Finiasi

Senivasi
Tiko Maciu
Seru
Waga Filimone
Koto
Tione Manu
Volau
Kubu

Vila
Soko
Apeti Tavou
Motu
Biu
Vili Taufa
Kubu

Volau
Motu
Vili Taufa
Tukana
Kubu
Senivasi

Seru
Laveti Seru
Motu
Vale
Semiti Bale
Ropate
Lepani
Tale Dautu
Senivasi

Semiti Bale
Motu
Puasa
Lutu

Wai
Kaci
Inoke
Motu
Galu
Vili Taufa
Tariasi
Tiko Macu
Tadu
Waqa Filimone
Koto

Figure 5.6. Yaqona Drinking Choices of the Linkers

Perhaps Motu was effective in his apparent capacity as a conveyer of information precisely because he did not attempt to manipulate people's opinions through information management. I think I missed seeing his role in the field because of my legal studies orientation; I was looking for hierarchical relationships and key roles identified with power and authority. But when a system is at least partly coordinate rather than superordinate in nature—and I suspect all are, if one takes a broad enough view—people like Motu who do not consciously try to exercise power and who are not thought of as powerful people may be extremely important.

LAW AND OTHER SYSTEMS OF SOCIAL CONTROL

In my analysis of conflict on Yanuyanu thus far, I have had little to say about law per se and its analogs that have been, by and large, the objects of legal ethnography. I have had to redefine the case into something hardly recognizable as such; I feel my approach is in the tradition of Malinowski's seminal *Crime and Custom in Savage Society* (1926), which as Epstein (1974) notes, has been regarded as "more of a contribution to general sociology" than to the literature of "tribal law and disputing" (p. 4). In the following, and in the concluding chapter I argue, to the contrary, that the approach I am using is a fruitful one of general application in the study of law, especially as law is seen in context of other social control institutions in society. Recent works by Conley and O'Barr (1990) and Merry (1990) emphasize the need to reconceptualize the case in legal anthropology along lines of discourse analysis.

6

Truth and Power, Reliance and Compulsion: Generating Communicative Causation in the Group

Mana!......E Dina!......A Muduo!
Power! ....Truth!......Finality!
Ritual formula chanted by all present
at the end of a *sevusevu.*

(Yanuyanu Island)

The description just presented (in Chapter 5) of the highly structured talk about conflict on Yanuyanu raises certain theoretical questions that need to be addressed at this point. In Chapter 2, I began the presentation of a theoretical rationale for ethnographic exploration of the communication system, arguing that the radical question in the ethnography of law and conflict is that of communicative causation.

To summarize my argument thus far, communicative causation is a problem for social science in general because humans live simultaneously in three interrelated worlds: inner, outer, and social (Figure 2.2). A "world" in this sense is defined by a specific regime of causation, and the science of each of the three must recognize the form of causation specific to the particular world it seeks to understand (Figure 2.1).

Language and communication arise at the interfaces of the worlds and allow their coordination. Although they are inextricably interrelated, the language system and the communication system should not be conflated. Language is generated by the interaction of the inner and social worlds, the individual mind and society, and—once established—it governs the operations of the inner world. A communication system, on the other hand, is generated by the interaction of the social and the outer world of physical reality. Indeed, in the case of the socialized individual the inner world no longer confronts the outer world the outer world directly but approaches it through the perceptual and cognitive filters of the socially and constructed language system and the constraining web of values and consequences—rewards and punishments—of the communication system.

Causation in the outer world is beyond the influence of human will; it is experienced as "A happens, then B happens" in invariable sequence. Causation in the inner world, too, is beyond rational control, being ruled by the Freudian primary process of human psychodynamics, which presumably is independent in its pattern of operation from the culture that arises in the social world.

This brings us to communicative causation, which governs the social world. I have argued for an ethnographic imperative in exploring the communication system, given that it arises in response to the unique social and physical ecology of the particular community and the specific character of its language system. In Chapter 3, 4, and 5. I have presented an ethnographic exploration of the communication system on Yanuyanu, which is a set of social identities (based on kinship relations among individuals and "caste" relations among groups) and most importantly, rules for the flow of messages among them. Analytically, I would separate the operations of the Yanuyanu system into two parts: *structural* communication or message flow that embodies the reality of the social world in its everyday, predictable operation (Chapters 3 and 4), and *control* or conflict communication that functions to repair and maintain that world and allow it to adapt to change (Chapter 5). That is the argument to this point.

But the theoretical connection between the communication system concept and the practical activities of villagers engaged in conflict management talk is still imprecise. I believe it is necessary to go further theoretically and explore in more detail the specific mechanism whereby the communication system of a community establishes a regime of communicative causation such that a predictable sequence of "A happens, then B" becomes entrenched in the social world. From the perspective of the individual actor, this means that the social world comes to resemble the outer, natural world in its predictability. The crucial difference between the two, however, which is not really apparent to the actor (or to the social scientist) precisely because of the similarity of the pattern, is that natural causation exists independently of human will, while communicative, social causation is the product of the communication system in operation. This communicative causation, in fact, is identical with the set of rules that establish social roles and govern message flow among them, including the shared conventions of meanings that mark out the range of interpretations allotted to the objects of exchange—including verbal performances—that constitute the content of the messages.

Rules, then, are the focus of investigation in understanding the communicative causation regime that obtains in the specific community. And rules, their formation, and their use are perhaps most salient in the part of the social process labeled disputing, which returns the discussion to the initial topic of conflict management. Particularly, this way of setting the problem of conflict management in a community underlines the question of the role of talk—understood as communication in the sense outlined thus far—plays in it. A persistent and rewarding question about that role, which I began with Chapter 2, is whether, or to what extent, talk *reflects* external reality in disputes or *constitutes* that reality through disputes.

In deference to Wittgenstein, these may be called the picture position and the game position, respectively. In using these terms, however, I am not referring precisely to Wittgenstein's own positions but to the general tenor of his very influential arguments. They are meant to indicate fundamental postures with regard to the relationship between language and various kinds of reality.

Wittgenstein indicates in a notebook entry (1979, p. 7e) that the idea for his picture theory occurred to him after considering how toy figures were used in a Paris traffic court to depict an auto accident. One gathers that each model represented a real car or person, and by manipulating the models the court officers were able to present a picture of the possible relationships among the real cars and people in the accident. In the same way, language "pictures" a possible reality. In his first great book, the *Tractatus,* Wittgenstein worked out the implications of this view of language and showed the severe limits it places on the use of language to represent reality in human endeavors. For one thing, much of the most important part of what people say when they discuss social relationships cannot be *said* at all, if saying is taken to mean stating verifiable propositions about real facts in the outer world.

---

[1] One way to look at the differences between, and the possible reconciliation of, Wittgenstein's two theories of language is to observe that, in terms of my argument (see Figure 2.2), his picture theory deals with only two worlds, inner and outer. In this, his first theory resembles Peirce's contribution to the philosophy of natural science, and the

With respect to the use of language in disputing or conflict management, one could argue that a version of the picture position, perhaps less severe than Wittgenstein's own, must lie behind the assumption that words can be used to represent what are generally called the facts—that is, what happened in an observable, physical sense. When it comes to rules and evaluative judgments, of course, language cannot be expected to perform in exactly the same way because the object referred to is not part of the real, material world but instead pertains to the social world. But even so, most people would say that a statement about rights and duties can have a definite meaning. Words can present a concept, idea, or rule—accurately or falsely—precisely because the idea, concept, or rule is something distinct from the language. In the dispute, then, two kinds of picturing or representing are going on, thoroughly mixed together. One kind traces ultimately to empirical reality, and the other to some kind of normative or definitional statement, but both can be examined critically for accuracy and efficiency.

To return to an incident I mentioned in the first chapter, when Epi told the other men that he had been chasing Vesu's cow all day because it had broken into his garden and damaged the crops, he was presenting a picture of both physical and social reality. The statements about the specific cow, and its entering and eating, concern real objects and events, while the assertion that it was *Vesu's* cow and *his* garden refer to basic, socially defined relationships of ownership that imply specific rights and obligations. What he said may have been true or false, or he may have exaggerated one way or the other. Also, the other men may or may not have understood clearly what he was talking about. These concerns—about the matching up between words and the realities they represent—presuppose a disjunctive theory of semantics that is basic to any kind of picture position. In such a theory there is a word, and then there is its meaning; it may be a general meaning—the cow as a type of animal—or a specific one—the black and white one with the crooked horn. The point is that the word and

---

major objection to the picture theory is that it is so limited. Because the social world is deleted, Wittgenstein has to conclude that one cannot really "talk" about events, concepts, and processes of the social world. Talk about them constitutes "nonsense."

Realizing that this is a serious problem, Wittgenstein then changes the focus in his subsequent game theory. But he still insists on only two worlds, and this time the inner world is lost to view. Working at the interface of the social and outer worlds, Wittgenstein has created a theory of communication, but he has great difficulty now dealing with language. This difficulty is indicated by the problems philosophers have had with his arguments about private language.

what it means are linked, either well or poorly. It is the job of language in disputes to do that linking and to do it with as little distortion as possible.

The game position, elucidated by Wittgenstein in his second great work, the *Philosophical Investigations,* rejects this semantic theory. Wittgenstein insists that we abandon the notion of meaning as something separate from the word. If we want to know about a word, we find out how it is used, not what meaning it is associated with. Language is a game, a social activity with rules created and enforced by the players, rather than a picturing process in which the ultimate question is the correspondence between language and the reality it represents or means. Instead, the rules of the game determine how a word is to be used, and that use is its meaning, to the extent that the word "meaning" survives—that is, can be used—at all.

Saussure (1966) decisively separated language from speech, conceptualized as the use of language in social settings. In doing so, he created two paths of investigation and chose to take the language system fork, leaving the more inclusive, anthropological study of talk in social context to others. From this point of view, Wittgenstein not only strode forth on the second path in delineating his game theory but brought the separation of the two paths sharply into question (cf. Benveniste, 1971).

It follows directly from the nondisjunctive, use theory of semantics underlying the game position that language actually constitutes much of what it "refers" to in social situations. When the object of discourse is definitional or normative in character, and when definition is equated with use, the way we talk about the object creates its meaning.

At the same time, the social, nonindividual character of the language game insures the necessary stability in use that allows communication to take place; completely idiosyncratic usage, like Humpty Dumpty's way of talking that Alice found so frustrating, is rejected by other players and has no impact on the rules of use. When there are few players in the total game, or again in a situation of mass communication where there are few players on the sending side and sufficient homogeneity on the receiving side to make the millions of simultaneous communication events involved similar to one another, the use/ meaning of words can change very quickly. Otherwise, when the relevant constitutive interactions are many, scattered in time and space, and largely unconnected, the rate of change can be very slow.

From the game perspective, the use of language by Epi and his fellow *yaqona* drinkers in their discussion of his problem has more to do with negotiating and creating social realities than with reporting or picturing them. The immediate social importance of the episode hinges on the rights and duties of Vesu as the owner of a cow and Epi as the owner of a garden. What these terms "mean" within the group—the expectations about behavior that one is allowed to express by statements such as "a cow owner must keep it tied up," and "no matter how careful the owner has been, he must pay for damage his cow does," under the rules of usage in effect—is directly shaped only by talk like that the men were engaged in. Changes in the physical objects referred to, gardens and cows, do not automatically result in changes in the rules; talk is clearly determinative in a direct sense facts, only indirectly so.

This pattern shows up more clearly when the distilled essence of the larger, informal process is displayed in legal institutions. The American legal realists, therefore, could assert that a legal rule is "what a judge says" rather than an entity with its own existence. From this perspective the legal process is clearly a type of language game with well articulated rules for regulating change and stability in the use of terms. H. L. A. Hart's influential work in jurisprudence can be looked at as a working out of the social rules that govern the law game, and MacCormick (1981) traces the cross-influences between Hart and the Oxford ordinary language philosophers (e.g., Ryle, 1949, and Austin, 1962), whose work parallels that of the later Wittgenstein.

Given the apparent analytic advantages of the constructivist position (see Brenneis, 1988), why should one continue to take seriously the view of language as something that should be critiqued in terms of the effectiveness with which it represents external realities such as facts and rules?

There are, I think, at least two reasons that the position reasserts itself in the analysis of language and disputing. One reason is that the participants in the dispute themselves are highly concerned with truth—the correspondence between language and reality, physical and social. Characteristically they are not content to accept as "fact" whatever the court says—or in the context of the Fijian village, whatever the group of relatives sitting around the *yaqona* bowl say. It matters that something is really so, and it is hard to remain a philosophical fact skeptic when one is personally involved in a dispute.

In their concern for facts, the disputants are confirming Peirce's observation that although we can know and talk about reality only indirectly—through the medium of images or signs—we *experience* reality directly. As I sit in a chair reading about the nature of matter and molecular structure, I may become convinced that if I concentrate very hard on the spaces between the particles of the matter involved, I can walk right through the wall. But when I try it, despite my sincere belief, I bounce off, suffering indignity if not injury. The resistance of physical reality, which I have just directly experienced, has taught me that my idea of reality, indirectly conveyed through words and thoughts, was false. Although Peirce was concerned only with two worlds, inner and outer, his analysis applies to social reality as well. I may sincerely believe that I have an absolute right to food, but if I don't pay the grocer, I may be arrested.

Science, according to Peirce, is a social response to the fundamental difference between knowledge of reality, which is always indirect, and the experience of it, which is always direct. Science allows us to have access not only to our own direct experience of physical reality but to that of others. Natural science is, in fact, a highly structured communication system that lets us make judgments about the truth and falsity of certain kinds of statements about the outer world, and law and other institutionalized conflict management practices do the same in specially limited ways that are adapted to the characteristics of the social world.

To understand why disputants act as they do, then, analysts have to take the use of language to picture reality—the question of truth, the correspondence of language and reality as participants perceive it— seriously. It is a construct held by the actors that influences their behavior and is reflected in institutional structure. One could no more understand law than science as a social process without reference to the idea or goal of truth.

A second, similar reason for being concerned with the picture position is that the analyst is also a participant in a larger sense. Often the importance of the research to the researcher and reader is also concerned with the question of truth. It is not just a matter of what the disputants think. For example, Gumperz (1982) shows how members of "nonstandard" speech communities may be systematically disserved by the legal system in a multiethnic society because of unnoticed prosodic details of their speech that result in routine misconstruction of their testimony. O'Barr and Conley have demonstrated similar potentially harmful effects of differences between the narrative styles of ordinary talk and that of legal discourse as O'Barr (1981) has that of differences between men's and women's talk.

From the game perspective, one could say that because of differences in socialization, not every participant is playing the legal language game by the same rules in these instances. But this becomes a problem precisely because it interferes with the picturing functions whereby facts are presented and the application of rules to the situation explained without distortion. The question of unfairness automatically expands the boundaries of the conflict discourse game because it refers to an external reality—the material, real-life disadvantages suffered by a class participants for reasons external to the understood rules and purposes of the game. This second question, then, can be seen to be concerned primarily with power, as the first is with truth. Presently (see Figure 6.2), I will develop the argument that these two concerns are the major dimensions of the social world and that the distinction between them can be related to that between language and communication.

It seems clear that both the representational and the constructivist views of the relationship between talk and social conflict have serious limitations if taken to their extremes. The picture or representational theorist cannot account for the process, so openly celebrated in the theory and practice of the common law tradition and clearly evident in other systems, whereby the law is created, sustained, and modified by the act of litigation itself. Law, as Giddens (1979) in his structuration theory says of social structure in general, not only controls, constrains, and enables people's actions as they litigate and as they conform to legal norms, it also at the same time exists by virtue of, and is shaped by, those same actions. In light of this observation, it seems very difficult to maintain that the disputing process, instantiated in communication events, does not in fact construct some of its own most important elements, specifically rules, values, and principles.

At the same time, a purely constructivist stance runs into an equally solid counterargument. It is hard to imagine a working conflict management system in which facts and preexisting rules were totally without weight and could be freely reconstructed with the immediate conflict discourse. Such an arbitrary system could probably be sustained within a group only by the exercise of overwhelming political and economic power. And in that case, too, the process would be reflecting an Orwellian external situation that it did not itself construct.

The sense in which legal systems—Westerns or non-Western, formal or informal—tend to construct facts derives from selection and decontextualization, but the same can be said for any system of representation at all. The facts as they happened and the facts as presented in briefs, testimony, and judgments are not identical. They could never be because one is an image of the other—a sign for it. And legal theories, like all theories, construct their own facts in the sense that they make certain aspects of reality salient and cause others to be ignored. It is only the details of the Fijian theories of property and injury that make the facts of where the cow went, what it did, whether it had been tied, whether the garden were fenced, and so on, the "facts" of the case.

LEVEL

	General (Rule)	Particular (case)
CYCLE Repre- sentation	Rules refer to social reality in order to make sense. They are valid only to the extent they represent categories of thought and patterns of action accurately.	Testimony about facts, assertions of rules and patterns of practice, and so on, are representations of facts and rules. They are true only if accurate.
Con- struction	Rules are applied through many individual cases, bringing about changes in social reality--construct-ing a general social reality.	Rules are applied to the particular case, construct-ing its facts. In governing future conduct of the parties, rules construct individuals' realities.

Figure 6.1.   Levels and Cycles in Conflict Management

LEVELS AND CYCLES IN CONFLICT MANAGEMENT PROCESSES

Clearly, then, both representation and construction—game theory and picture theory—are necessary parts of an analysis of a conflict management process. In order to avoid confusion in seeing them in relation to one another, one must recognize the cyclical nature of conflict management itself and distinguish two levels at which the cycles operate. Figure 6.1 identifies the two basic stages in the cycle of conflict management as representation and construction. The two levels at which the cycles operate are the general and the particular; the former is the level of the rule that purports to govern all similar situations, and the latter that of the specific conflict case in which the rule is sought to be applied.

The upper-left box in Figure 6.1, indicating the application of the picturing cycle at the general level, raises the issue of representation in the general sense—not whether the specific picture of events presented by the participant in the particular conflict management event is true or false, but whether the rule is capable of allowing an accurate picture to be formed, that is, whether it is valid or invalid as a rule, however it might be applied in the specific case. A rule, in other words, is always a picture of the situation it seeks to govern, whether that situation exists in fact or in the imagination of the legislator as a desired future state of affairs. A rule that an owner must keep his cow confined assumes that there are cows, that confinement of them is possible, that there is such a relationship as "ownership" possible between cows and people.

The sense in which a rule is capable of representing a reality actually or potentially external to itself—that is, the sense in which it is "realistic" in its potential application—is a parallel to the more general relationship of total cultural knowledge to external reality. Being part of that larger picture, the rules used in social control must be generally consistent with cultural theories and tenents.

The commercial traffic in imaginary tree sprites that Oliver (1955) reports among the Siuai of Bougainville could give rise to rules concerning their ownership, transfer, implied warranties, and so on. Such rules, in their application to disputes that might arise among the Siuai, would provide within the disputing discourse the vehicles for representation of external facts such as the size and character of the sprite at issue. The object being represented, however, is in this instance itself a construction arising from the discourse of Siuai metaphysics. The dispute, however, because of its topic, becomes part of that larger metaphysical discourse, simultaneously confirming and to a greater or lesser extent altering the construct in question. The relationships of constructing and picturing would be the same, of course, even if the object were a more universally recognized one such as a house timber or a pig. An analyst external to the situation might raise the question of whether the tree or the tree sprite within it is "real" or not and whether reference to one is representation and to the other construction. But that question involves an element of perspective, and the issue of perspective is raised by the multiple structure of cycles in any conflict management institution.

The longer cycle, general in scope and including many individual disputing episodes that bear upon the practice or set of expectations at issue, concerns the formation of rules. That formation always involves construction, but the necessity that rules—like all statements within established forms of social discourse—refer to a reality consistent with social knowledge and the exigencies of nature, inevitably raises a question of representation or picturing. That question concerns representation in the general sense of creating the conditions in which specific, case-level representation can take place. In this longer, institutional scale cycle too, a general form of construction takes place through a societal language game.

In the larger sense each instance of its use in a conflict management event recreates the rule and makes it conform to the realities
represented by the particular case. It is in context of this larger cycle,
in which generalized picturing and constructing go on, that the
conflict management process can be said to reflect or represent and at
the same time, being an instance of it, help to construct the enduring
external realities of the political and economic regimes of the society.
From this perspective, disputing discourse both represents (in the
general sense) *and* helps construct what Brenneis calls "'real action'
going on elsewhere in the sociopolitical sphere," which is construction
in the general sense, shown in the bottom, left box in Figure 6.1.

Figure 6.2 illustrates the stages involved in a conflict management
cycle and indicates the points at which picturing and construction
become issues. The movement indicated from social practice to rule
and then back to social practice is perhaps less circular than spiral in
nature, with the practice returned to being modified each time. The
two stages of movement, from practice to rule and from rule to
practice, are each dominated by a different principle of action.

The first is characterized by and draws its vitality from the
principle of reliance, while the second concerns compulsion in some
form. The primary concern of the first stage is that the rule conform to
the existing or desired practice, and therefore picturing or representing in the general, potential sense is the salient communication issue.

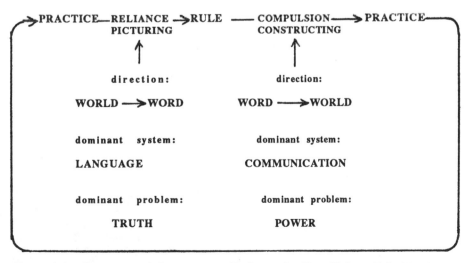

Figure 6.2. Picturing and Constructing Cycles in Conflict: Shifting Polarities in
World Wide Influence

In the second stage, the problem is making practice conform to the rule, and construction is the issue.

Whether people engaged in conflict management are seen as picturing or constructing—both inherent in the larger communication process—depends on the direction of the stage in the cycle: from practice to rule or from rule to practice. Put another way, reliance is the social psychological and ethical force that turns is (practice, whether preexisting or projected) to ought (rule). In order to accomplish this transformation, practice (reality) must be represented or pictured within rule (language). Compulsion, the other side of the coin, runs from *ought* to *is,* language to reality, rule to practice. The two major axes of the social world are here represented: truth and power. The first is dominated by the language system, its potential and its accurate application to aspects of the natural and social world external to it, while the second is dominated by the communication system that governs, through its unique set of social identities and rules for message flow among them, "who says what to whom through what channel with what effect," as Lasswell (1948) put it.

The specific case or instance of conflict discourse is one point among many that may be taking place in the society at which the construction of social meaning may be inched along, only culminating in significant change over a long span of time. The individual conflict case, therefore, bears the relationship of the particular to the general to the larger, institutional scale process. It is the relationship of the specific court case to the evolving common law or, in the context of the Fijian village, that of particular episodes of conflict and communication about conflict to rules or scenarios generally accepted by public opinion. The case is one element within the larger cycle, which may aggregate the social and ideational impact of many such instances.

In its internal structure, too, the case like the larger system is a cycle from practice to rule and back to practice, but the principles and forms of communication involved are particular rather than general. The narrative discourse of the case is concerned in large part with presenting an accurate picture of the specific events and states of affairs that led to the conflict. At the same time the application of rules, which is essentially a constructing process, permeates the entire event, strongly influencing the selection and interpretation of raw events, and forming the story line that invests the narrative with meaning and social impact. Picturing and constructing are both strongly represented, therefore, in the specific case just as they are in the larger cycle of conflict management.

In some sense, as illustrated in the case cycle, picturing can be reduced to a phase within the larger constructive process. When, for example, a participant refers to, reports, and represents facts in language, those facts are often not independent or natural but are, like the Siuai tree sprites, themselves the constructed products of encompassing forms of social discourse. Talking about something that is created by, and exists only by virtue of, talk inevitably becomes part of the constructing process and shapes the thing referred to. But this kind of constructing still appears to the participants to be picturing—and functions within the scope of the case as picturing—when the object is somehow protected from immediate modification by the talk. Such protection may stem from explicit metarules that limit the overt modification of certain privileged concepts or statements—refusing to accept as valid any changes that have not been made in a certain way or by certain people. In less formal systems it may simply be the public nature of the process that inhibits change; public opinion operates as a sort of normative flywheel that is difficult to alter once set in motion. In either case, it is clear that some amount of micro construction is inevitable—as in the "interstitial legislation" Hart (1961) refers to as part of the judicial process of applying rules to specific cases. No rule can be formulated in such a way that every future application is anticipated, and therefore each new application must constitute a partial rewrite. The point, however, is that freewheeling modification is dampened, and the critical question is the preponderance of the direction of influence: Is talk largely causing the object to change, or is the object causing the talk to conform to its dictates?

CONFLICT MANAGEMENT AS A FUNCTION OF THE COMMUNICATION SYSTEM

The communication system, as I have shown by example in the preceding ethnographic chapters, is a system of roles, defined on Yanuyanu by kin relationships at the individual level and by a castelike division of function at the group to group level, and rules governing the flow of messages among them. In its operation, the communication system produces social institutions—the social practices that constitute the economics, law, religion, family life, and so on—of the group.

All this activity, which is the substance of the social world, is possible only to the extent that messages can be depended upon to produce predictable effects within the community. That is, it depends upon the establishment of a regime of communicative causation. As I have argued earlier, this form of causation, which simulates some characteristics of natural causation, arises from the cycle from practice to rule and back to practice that employs the processes of reliance and compulsion and requires the language functions of picturing and construction.

Jakobson (1960), Malinowski (1923), and others have pointed out that language serves a number of functions, not just that of representation. For example, language focuses outward on external reality to serve the function of representation, but turns inward upon itself to accomplish the act of poetry. Phatic communion serves to maintain social relationships but does not really convey external information.

Similarly, the communicative system serves a variety of structural functions, including social control. In the following, final chapter, I tentatively explore the complexity of the social situation—a complexity that is perhaps diagnostic of Western industrial democratic society—that arises when multiple communication systems, whether allocated to different spheres of social life or in competition with one another—coexist within a community. I argue that this "modern" condition of life is beginning to take root even in the traditional villages of Fiji.

7

The Power and Pleasures of Talk: Control Communication, Societal Conflict, and Formative Context

I want [the Fiji Indians] to stay here It will bo a big challenge for us to convert them to Christianity ... we either go that way, or they convert us and we all become heathens ... I don't think they will resent it, because all we are trying to do is the same thing that the missionaries did here in Fiji when we were cannibals and heathens. (S. Rabuka quoted in Dean & Ritova 1988)

In the preceding chapters I have alternated between the ethnograhic present of 20 years ago on a small island in Southern Lau and the past/ future/present, synchronic realm of social theory. In concluding I will advance to the "current events present" of the recent-past/near-future and, at the same time, move from the local conflict talk of the village to national and international conflict discourse. In doing this, I am addressing the question, presented in the preface, of linking the small and the large of discourse analysis. Regimes of communicative causation, generated by conflict talk that is framed in each case by specific communication systems, span the gap between the precise form of a local conversation about conflict in the village and the broad forms of conflict discourse that shape the course of history at the national and regional levels.

KINSMEN, CHIEFS, AND CHRISTIAN SOLDIERS

On May 14, 1987, a small group of well-drilled soldiers wearing ski masks and armed with automatic pistols entered the Fijian Parliament chamber and arrested the government members. Their action was the first, decisive event in a tightly planned sequence designed to deliver the supreme political authority of the nation into the hands of a lieutenant-colonel of the Royal Fiji Military Forces, Sitiveni Rabuka.

The coup followed a historic national parliamentary election in which for the first time the political party identified with the indigenous Fijians lost control and was replaced by a coalition government.[1] The coalition was formed between the major opposition party, which is dominated by the Fiji Indians, and a new labor party led by an indigenous Fijian who opposed the traditional leadership. Although the new Prime Minister, Dr. Bavadra, was an ethic Fijian, a vocal and militant opposition arose that proclaimed the new government a threat to the constitutional rights of the indigenous Fijians. Colonel Rabuka argued that his action in removing the coalition government was necessary to prevent bloody conflict between the two major ethnic communities in Fiji: indigenous Fijians and Fiji Indians.

Having consolidated control throughout the country, Colonel Rabuka eventually allowed a civilian government to form for purposes of rewriting the Fijian constitution to insure the overtly stated purpose of the coup. Couched in politicolegal terms, these objectives were to guarantee absolute political control and exclusive ownership of most of the land to indigenous Fijians and to prevent power from falling into the hands of Fiji Indians or any coalition between Fiji Indians and dissident indigenous Fijians who might reject traditional chiefly authority. By September 26, however, the colonel felt that forces of the status quo ante were reasserting themselves, and the country was sliding back into a "moderate" posture of compromise on issues of political control and land ownership. Accordingly, he executed a second coup, proclaiming himself head of state and revoking the original 1970 constitution altogether. On October 6th, at midnight, the exact anniversary of Fiji's emergence from colonial control by the British and entry into the Commonwealth, Rabuka proclaimed Fiji a republic, severing ties with the Crown.

The two military coups in Fiji constituted a shocking turn of events

---

[1] In an earlier election, the Fijian-dominated Alliance party was defeated, but the Fiji Indian party, the Federation, was unable to form a viable government, and the Fijian Governor General called for a new election, which the Alliance was able to win.

in the Pacific. Fiji, since its independence, had emerged as a showcase of economic development and democracy in the islands. According to conventional wisdom, the other island nations, all of which aside from Papua New Guinea are smaller than Fiji and have fewer resources, range from economic basket cases to marginal countries in need of permanent aid relationships with donor countries such as Australia, New Zealand, Great Britain, or the United States. Fiji, however, had begun to make important strides in increasing the range of its exports from agricultural products and raw materials to manufactured goods such as clothing and furniture. Tourism was also developing in what seemed a healthy, well-controlled way. An important factor in Fiji's economic development was the presence in the country of the Fiji Indians, most of whose ancestors came to the islands as indentured sugar cane plantation workers under the British. Constituting at present about one-half the population of the country, the Fiji Indians as a population segment tend to be well educated, highly motivated, and a valuable source of entrepreneurial and bureaucratic talent.

With specific regard to the dual ethnic nature of the country, pre-coup Fiji was also given high marks within the region and beyond for the moderate, biracial character of its political process. On the basis of its skillful handling of the "ethnic problem," in fact, Fijian political leadership had achieved a solid reputation for statesmanship that enhanced its regional influence. In particular, the long-time Prime Minister of Fiji, Ratu Mara, had been accorded a high level of respect in regional, Commonwealth, and United Nations circles.

The military takeover, then, and what seemed a total collapse of the ethnic modus vivendi came as a rude shock to the regional political community. Extreme events might have been expected in the other, more troubled island countries, but not in moderate, progressive Fiji. In a way, the coups were an affront to the region's faith in Western style liberal democracy and market-driven development.

But as shocking as the events may have been, they could hardly have been said to have been unanticipated. The potential for civil conflict in Fiji had been a byword in the Pacific since independence from Britain made it an issue. On the one side an ideology of indigenous rights portrayed the Indian citizens of Fiji as foreign usurpers who, if unchecked by constitutional restraints, would take over and dominate the country to the detriment of the indigenes—a historical pattern observed in Hawaii, New Zealand, and Australia already. On the other side, the basic Western sense of distributive justice articulated by Aristotle—that those who are equal in one dimension will demand equality in all things—strikes any outside observer: How long can citizens of Indian extraction be content with a legal system under which ownership of over 80 percent of the land is guaranteed to their indigenous compatriots?

In the explosion of analysis and explanation that has followed the coups, including extensive foreign and domestic media coverage, a large number of academic books and articles (see Lal & Peacock, 1990; MacDonald, 1990), and of course highly animated conversation throughout the region, a number of distinct causes for the coups have been postulated. For example, cultural conflict, competition for land, economic conflict, and conflict over political control between the two major ethnic groups in Fiji have been heavily emphasized. Also, East-West global conflict has been cited, with the idea that the U.S. CIA engineered the coups because of fear that the new coalition government would take a nonaligned stance like India's and lean toward the Soviet Union. Also, class struggle has been argued for as the root cause by some observers who discount ethnic divisions and see the conflict as one between urban workers and the ruling elite. Traditional political conflict among the indigenous Fijian power blocks—traceable to internal wars that were brought to an end only with cession to Great Britain—has been implicated by some commentators, while others have argued that the outgoing Alliance party government had been shielding its leaders, including the former Prime Minister, from the exposure of massive corruption over the years, and the coups were necessary to prevent the new coalition government from taking action on these crimes.

Most analysts have taken the stance that there is no *one* cause of the coups. Like any problem of social analysis, this one involves enumerating all the convergent causes and examining their interactions. All have insisted on assigning weight to the various factors, however, emphasizing some reasons for the coups and discounting others. Thus, many writers, journalists, or academics have fastened on ethnic conflict as the most prominent cause, portraying the other factors as playing a facilitating role. Others have strongly emphasized class conflict and have discounted ethnic differences.

To this list of causes of the coups I would like to add one that, although mentioned (see Garrett, 1990), has not been generally emphasized. Religion, and more particularly a phenomenon that can be identified as religious fundamentalism, has played an important role in the coups.

The overt part played by religion has been amply reported, but I believe it has not been given its due weight. For example, Colonel Rabuka himself is a Methodist lay preacher and has used religious arguments extensively to explain his actions. In a heavily autobiographical book written with two journalists (Dean & Ritova, 1988), and in a film produced for Fijian audiences, Rabuka has portrayed his actions as based on direct, personal communication from God. He has indicated that he has been chosen by God to accomplish a specific mission on behalf of the indigenous Fijians. Furthermore, a segment of the established Methodist church in Fiji has supported such an interpretation of the coups, and overt actions have been taken such as the erection of roadblocks by religiously inspired civilians for the purpose of preventing work, sports, social activity, and excessive travel on Sundays (Garrett, 1990). In isolated cases mosques and Hindu temples have been attacked by young men who said they were acting in the interests of religious purity. The post-coup governments have distanced themselves from such volunteer activity, but they have supported the establishment of Fiji as a "Christian Republic." Rabuka, in his book and in interviews, has stated that his aim is to convert the Fiji Indians to Christianity, identifying them as "heathens," and likening their conversion to that of the Fijians themselves under the British.

Most social scientists and journalists who have analyzed the coups, I believe, may have largely discounted the apparent religious dimension of the coup situation because they see it as mere rhetoric and justification on the part of the actors. In this sense it is seen as the equivalent of the "God, Mother, and Apple Pie" talk of American politicians, whose real motivations are distinctly related to money and power.

I would argue that for a substantial segment of the Fiji population religion has a different status than that it enjoys in the mainstream of Western democracies.[2] Indigenous Fijian society is still strongly organized around traditional, total relationship systems, kinship and the chiefly hierarchy, that I have portrayed as communication systems in the previous chapters. Indigenized protestant Chrisitianity has also asserted itself as an alternate communication or relationship system. Before cession to the British, Fiji, engaged in intense warfare that was resulting in the formation of larger and larger alliances and confederations, can be seen as a traditional tribal society seeking an

---

[2] Of course, there are those among the populations of the industrialized democracies who do accept religion as a total system of communication (see Greenhouse, 1986). The rise of the religious right wing in American politics during the Reagan years is an example of the prevalence of this antimodern communication system and is evidence of the fact that the impulse toward the total system is not confined to "traditional" societies. My argument here is simply that such systems are much closer to the mainstream in Fiji than in the United States, for example, where are embraced by small splinter groups.

overarching total relationship system that would allow political and
economic integration along feudal lines.

Contact with European nations at first accelerated but finally
interrupted that process and created a situation in which a new kind of
total relationship system was needed—one that went beyond kinship
and chief-vassal bonds to encompass new, more global societal hori-
zons. Christianity offerred such a total system, as Fijians interpreted
it. Under British rule, this new relationship system could not come to
full flower, although along with the chiefly system it was strongly
reinforced as an instrument of indirect rule. With independence,
however, its logic as a total system could begin to reassert itself. When
religion seeks to become a total system of social communication—
governing economics, politics, artistic expression, and every other
aspect of life—the phenomenon of religious fundamentalism has
appeared.

From this perspective, the presence of a large and powerful population segment that cannot be assimilated into the total system—and in
fact adheres to the pluralistic, nontotal pattern of modernism—cannot
be tolerated. As Rabuka jokingly put it, "either we convert them or we
all go the other way and they convert us to heathenism" (Dean &
Ritova, 1988, p. 121).

The interrelationships among the contending total systems of
communication involved in Fijian society present an interesting pattern of opposition and alliance. Indigenized Christianity and the
chiefly system are fundamentally in conflict, I would argue, but they
have been forced into an alliance against modern pluralism. To
portray itself as a total institution, the church needs to appropriate
traditional culture, which includes the chiefly complex. To secure a
toehold in the modernized societal context forced upon them by
Western contact, the chiefs need to portray themselves as upholders of
the globally accepted—or at least accepted by the new High Chief, the
Queen of England—values and morals represented by the church.

The coups, in which a nonchief claiming the Christian God as his
source of authority has rudely stripped power from the highest
traditional chiefs—the Governor General was a chief of the highest
traditional rank, and that of the former prime minister was only
slightly lower—dramatizes the conflict between two systems that
need each other but can never really merge. The church allocates
power one way, and the chiefly system another, and the two, being total
in ambition, cannot agree to the usual spiritual/temporal split of
domains. The third total system in contention, kinship, blocked from
ultimate victory by the limitations of its own biologically grounded
premises, is still powerful enough to act as a broker between the other

two. Colonel Rabuka repeatedly overrode the chiefs in his actions and then, using the traditional ritual of apology, *i soro*, which is grounded in the kinship regime, sought to coopt their authority by reinstating their moral leadership.

THE CONTROL COMMUNICATION PERSPECTIVE

Elsewhere (Arno, 1985a), I have argued for a broad, discourse-centered model of conflict management institutions that makes analytical distinction between structural communication and control communication. The argument is that the everyday, or at least normal, message flow in society, structured by shared meanings and sets of interrelated social identities, constitutes structural communication. In Chapters 3 and 4, I have provided examples of structural communication at the group-to-group and individual levels as its constitutes the normal political and economic order of village life on Yanuyanu. Control communication, portrayed in Chapter 5, is a specific response to conflicts that arise in the course of normal social process. Some of these conflicts, such as those that derive from autonomy struggles between parent and child or between fissioning lineage segments, are built in to the structure of everyday life and cannot be eradicated, while others are more contingent in nature. Control communication requires its own institutional entrenchment in order to deal with the conflicts it seeks to repair, and characteristically every society has a variety of such institutions, partly in contention and partly complementary to one another. From the theoretical perspective I have urged in this book, each control communication institution in a society is a distinct form of conflict discourse. In stable, traditional societies, the dominant form of conflict communication is congruent with structural communication and tends to reinforce it in operating on conflicts. For example, kinship and the chiefly system of group relations dominate life on Yanuyanu, and the most powerful form of conflict discourse, described in Chapter 5 as a highly institutionalized set of practices that govern how relatives talk about conflict, grows out of and reinforces that regime.

Like all control communication institutions, the kinship centered system of conflict talk on Yanuyanu imposes its influence on structural communication in two ways: by providing a set of categories that define or redefine the substance of the conflict issue, and by enforcing a pattern of interaction through its procedural rules that govern the way participants in the conflict can communicate with one another. For example, the ritual apology, *i soro,* which is an integral part of the kinship control system, prescribes a set of roles that the participants must take, and those roles dramatically enact a powerfully hierarchical relationship pattern. As I have argued, hierarchy is instantiated in one-way communication in which one party is restrained and the other is free (see Figure 4.2). In the *i soro,* the penitent remains silent while the *yaqona* or whale's tooth he or she has brought is presented by a spokesman. The person offering the apology also looks down, cutting off visual communication, and must be dressed in a conservative, nonassertive way. Meanwhile the person to whom the apology is directed may respond directly—sometimes even sending the other person away angrily, although eventually the apology must be accepted.

The *i soro,* therefore, enacts through its own ritual procedure, the key, ordering pattern of structural communication on Yanuyanu: hierarchy. After it has been performed, the participants in the event may resume their normal, prescribed ways of interacting. And while the *i soro* itself does not provide for discussion of the substantive issues of the conflict, the talk that has gone on in the village preceding and following the ritual does allow for full exploration of the problem. It is in this forum part of the process that the categories and behavior rules of the kinship control system define the problem and assert a way of resolving it.

Of course, on Yanuyanu there are other control communication instititutions that might be appealed to to deal with conflicts, but they are subordinate. For example, the national legal system may be called upon, as may the bureaucratic rulemaking apparatus of the state. The church also eagerly offers itself as a structuring template for relationships, but in the end the kinship/chiefly system successfully imposes its own influence.

For other societies, as in the United States, the law has a much more powerful position, but even here there are a variety of other control communication systems in addition. The mass news media, for example, play an important role in American societal conflicts (Arno, 1985a), as do other institutionalized ways of talking about and managing conflicts such as religion, medicine, and social science. The particular mix of control communication institutions, and their interrelationships, constitute a specific formative context, to use Unger's (1988) term for the persisting set of ideas and practices that operate to keep the political, economic, and social configuration of a society within particular limits.

Societies that encourage change in many aspects of life may also encourage a lack of congruence between structural communication in a particular sphere of life and the control communication institution that operates upon it. In areas of social change, therefore, such as those involving gender or racial relationships in contemporary America, the law may intrude in areas, like the workplace or the university classroom, that have been left to more congruent, informal control institutions in more quiescent times dominated by the status quo.

THE COUP AS SOCIETAL CONFLICT

While some conflicts are local, limited in scope, and affect only a small number of people, others are quite complex and extensive. Conflicts in society can be looked at as distributed in terms of time, space, participants, and the control communication institutions they involve. When a conflict issue comprehends a large number of subconflicts that are linked by topic but differentiated in the other dimensions, it can be considered a societal conflict. For example, the AIDS epidemic in the United States involves innumerable conflict episodes involving individuals, private companies, schools, government agencies, and professional groups. In various situations the problem may be viewed in economic, legal, medical, political, or ethical terms and the corresponding control communication institutions will be invoked—or will impose themselves—to define the situation and point toward some restructuring of societal routines to manage the conflict.

When a genuine societal conflict presents itself, the various contending and complementary control discourses of a community swarm into action, attacking the issue like elements of an ideational immune system. At the individual, micro level of conflict talk, participants can be seen to invoke them, while from a societal perspective they seem to arise spontaneously and inevitably.

The coups, as soon as they became known to the various audiences involved—urban and rural, national and international—immediately provoked an energetic stream of talk, analysis, and commentary. Each of the lines of argument I mentioned above—put forward in the mass media, academic journals, and private conversations, and which interpreted the events in distinct frameworks of causation and resolution—represents a form of control communication discourse attempting like an army of rhetorical phagocytes to engulf the issue, digest it, and render it harmless.

But control communication institutions, and regimes of social causation they grow out of, do not merely react to events that take place. As part of the cycle between practice and rule and back to practice again (see figure 6.2), they precipitate events as well. They are part of the calculus, consciously attended to or not, of the formulation of goals and anticipation of the reaction the event will evoke.

To illustrate my point, I will refer to a communication event, concerned with a widely recognized conflict issue, that I recorded on Yanuyanu some 16 years before the first coup, but which cannot be viewed as totally unconnected, in context of societal conflict discourse, with those later events.

The event was a debate performed for my tape recorder by Tui and Rusiate. Debate is an integral part of the local economy of conflict communication on Yanuyanu and is a frequent element of yaqona drinking sessions. A variety of joking, it allows cross-cousins to display their skills in verbal dueling without being held accountable for what they say. The prosodic details of its performance mark the place of the particular debate along a continuum from serious *vakaturaga,* discussion to the all-out verbal assault and battery of personal joking attacks (Arno, 1990).

In this case the joking is of a mild variety, with few pointed personal illusions. Tui opens it by posing a question (see the transcript in Appendix A), and the expectation is that the two will take opposing sides and attempt to discredit one anothers' arguments and win the debate by their own persuasiveness. In terms of the perspective developed in this chapter, the two participants make their points by invoking several distinct control communication discourse systems.

Although the communication system based on kinship and the traditional intergroup relationships of the chiefly complex is dominant and pervasive on Yanuyanu, there are other ways of construing and prescribing relationships within the island community. One is the incompletely worked out, only partly legitimated system based on the polar concepts of *rarama* (light) and *butobuto* (darkness). This way of organizing social relationships, which I have referred to a number of times in describing conversations on Yanuyanu in previous chapters, can be understood as a body of abstract concepts and categories concerning modernity and progress, with specific implications for roles and communications patterns.

Thus, for example, Tui could say (in Chapter 5) that in a situation of true *rarama* members of a *yavusa* would speak frankly to one another and settle the question of each's contribution to the tea for the group during the Christmas/New Year *kana vata*. And when Master Manu, a school teacher with no relatives on the island, entered a dark house where a group of men were drinking yaqona on a chilly evening, the question of the way strangers were to be treated under the contrasting social regimes was raised jokingly. Manu was wearing a long overcoat, and one man remarked that the magnificence of the coat could be compared only to those of the "Topasi" men in Suva, a reference to the Topaz rubbish company whose employees wear long dust coats during their collection activities. Another said: "What a lucky thing for you that this is an era of *rarama*. In the old days of *butobuto,* a stranger like you would not have left this house alive wearing such a coat."

The concept of *rarama,* with its vaguely defined communication system, draws its authority, tenuous as it is, from a specific failure of the traditional system, namely its inherent localization. Basing patterns of communication that operate to instantiate cooperation, authority, and controlled competition only on marriage and descent is so limiting that the traditional system had to evolve larger scale, group-to-group relationships. For example, the relationship of *turaga* to *vanua* served at an island or regional level, while the *tau vu* system linked regions and specific localities in different regions throughout the Fiji islands even where unifying chiefly authority was absent. In Lau, military conquests and alliances—a function of the chiefs' interrelationships, a *turaga-turaga* system—created a hierarchical system of relations among the islands such that people from the lower-ranked islands had to behave in ways that displayed their inferiority when they visited higher-ranked islands.

But while the traditional system may have been able in this way to evolve into a potentially national system of communication, how was it to deal with the sudden, unignorable appearance of people from completely outside that system? How was the 19th-century Fijian to communicate, in a pattern that satisfied the functional needs of an acceptable social framework, with Europeans and Indians?

From this perspective, the importance of the Christian church as an alternative communication systems is clear. Military force alone is not a sufficient mode of domination in a colonial situation. In order to establish consensual, social hegemony as well as physical rule, colonial nations are often motivated to establish their own religions as a common, incorporating communication system. From the Fijian side, a similar but mirror image impulse propels the evolution of a system that is related to the traditional communication system but offers integrative scope. As Kaplan's (1990) analysis of the *Tuka* movement in Viti Levu shows, such a system exerts a reordering effect not only outwardly, establishing a way of incorporating the British and the Europeans world, but also inwardly, challenging traditional patterns.

In this way, the Wesleyan church in Fiji has also been recreated in some degree by Fijians in order to establish a relatively seamless communication system that prescribes patterns of interaction within the village, constituting regimes of authority and cooperation, and at the same time places the Fijian in the context of world society. In true

Fijian fashion, the village church is organized along strictly hierarchical and strongly competitive lines.

Parishioners seeking to participate in the alternative system of social identities offered by the church enter at the bottom grade and, by maintaining strictly enforced rules of behavior and demonstrating the acquisition of religious knowledge, advance to higher status levels, including that of the *dauvunau* or lay preachers, who are privileged to speak from the pulpit. At the apex of the organization, the ordained minister oversees the functions of the church, which are often forwarded through controlled competition.

Church music on Yanuyanu, for example, is provided by four choirs, each with its own leadership and organization. Once a month, at the special *Polotu* service, the choirs sing competitively against one another, being judged by a panel of church elders on a number of dimensions that include costume as well as musical performance. In fund raising events, too, groups compete to give as much as possible, and the amounts are announced to the entire assembly to appropriate praise.

Tui, pursuing one of his favorite conversational themes, told me that formerly the children in Sunday school were asked to compete with one another to see who could bring in the most money over the year. Tui said that he was incensed by this practice, which resulted in his children asking for more and more money each Sunday, and which he took to be ideologically incorrect as well. Accordingly, he wrote to the head of the church in Lau complaining and suggesting that instead the children should be asked to complete in the number of bible verses they could learn. He reported that he had triumphed in this particular battle against church hypocrisy: the head of the church had sent word that Tui was right and that the competition should be changed.

Rarama as a control communication institution has a complex relationship with the Christian church. The church as a communication system attempts to borrow legitimacy from the broader force of modernity by claiming that it is not only an integral part of Western industrial democratic life but the very foundation of that way of life. But at the same time the indigenized Fijian church is, for many adherents, a total system that does not accept the discourse pluralism characteristic of modernity.

Both Tui and Rusiate, in their debate, refer implicitly to the broader, pluralistic control discourse of *rarama* as modernization rather than to the fundamentalist church version. Neither man is a church supporter. Rusiate is perhaps a bit of an intellectual skeptic, and he enjoys homebrew drinking too much to accept the church's teetotal prohibitionary stance. Tui's family is very near the apex of the traditional chiefly hierarchy in Lau, and many of his comments can be interpreted as reflecting a resentment of nonchiefs using the church as source of authority. Opening the debate, Tui says: "Rusiate, what do you think...if this coming election takes place [and] the Indians win...what might you think would happen in Fiji in the future"(A:1-4)?

Rusiate attempts to stake out a position of *rarama* from which to argue. If that were to happen, he says, "I would be disposed to trust in the gentlemen of India because they are educated gentlemen" (A:6-7). "Many of them are lawyers" (A:7-8), he comments, although I am not sure if this is intended as ironic or not. Having taken the high road of *rarama,* Rusiate then prompts Tui to take the contrary, kinship/ chiefly perspective. "What do you think, Tui," he says, "isn't there something that they will cause trouble about at present in Fiji" (A:14-18)?

But Tui refuses and takes the *rarama* argument even further. "I agree with you," he says. "I think it appears that it is not a concern. It will be excellent if our kinsmen the Indians take the leadership here in our nation of Fiji. I know that we are in accord...that we know one another's customs" (A:19-24). He goes on to assert that "if some other races of people were to lead us...Indian, or European, or Chinese, I think...my complete belief is...that it would be wonderful. It will be completely the same if only they are well educated, with many earned academic degrees. But I would like to hear if there are some other thoughts that you are thinking" (A:26-32)?

Now Rusiate must take the position of the traditionalist, if the two-sided, competitive form of the debate is to be respected. Both he and Tui like to portray themselves as progressive and modern in general, contrasting themselves with the backward, ignorant elements of the village. Perhaps this is why he attacks Tui lightly at this point—to show his annoyance at being placed in this position. "It is true that I spoke consistently with what you said" (A:33-34), he begins. He then notes parenthetically that Tui's defense of education is understandable. "It's true that you also are a well educated person" (A:34-35), he says, but this is a joking attack because Tui is still famous in the village for his spectacularly poor showing as a schoolboy 35 years earlier.

At this point, Rusiate abandons the *rarama* position that elevates education and devalues kinship and chiefly hierarchy. In fact, he attacks the line of argument that he initiated and refers to the benefits of education with irony. "Nevermind, if you please, their wisdom," he says, "that they will exercise so nicely to govern" (A:45-46). Attacking the Fiji Indians directly, Rusiate says that "this is a race...we know their reputation as a group who hide what they are feeling inside" (A:45-46). Rusiate goes on to argue that if the Fiji Indians take power they will end up changing the laws that govern the Native Lands Trust, which guarantees Fijian communal ownership of most of the land in the country. This is "a frightening thing to us *i taukei*" (A:46-47), he declares.

Rusiate goes on to portray the land as the firm foundation of the indigenous Fijians—their only, last, and best hope for survival (e.g., A:51-54). He contrasts the Fiji Indians with the indigenous Fijians, arguing that the Indians are able to make a lot of money in business because they are so well educated, while the Fijians have only their land (A:55-57).

In responding, Tui at first admits everything that Rusiate has said, claiming that once the Fiji Indians are elected to power, it will be impossible for the *taukei* to regain control or to prevent the reversal of the native lands trust policy (A:63-69). This apparent collapse of his opponent's argument seems to catch Rusiate off balance, and he makes a rather unconnected, mumbled response (A:70-71).

Whether as a strategic move or simply a reflection of his train of thought, Tui suddenly comes up with a rather creditable modernist counter argument. He points out that in a parliamentary democracy the opposition party doesn't simply go out of existence. The Alliance will still be a powerful force, he argues, capable of continual confrontation, *veisaqa*, in the parliamentary process. His conclusion is that there is no need to panic, even if the Federation party does win the election (A:72-81).

Rusiate is now forced to respond in modernist terms, attempting to display his superior sophistication and knowledge of parliamentary politics. His argument now is that the role of the opposition in any parliamentary system is a weak one, one of subservience to the Government. Whereas before both men had used the global inclusive possessive pronoun, *noda,* as in referring to *noda vanua* or *noda matanitu,* "our land" or "our government", which implies a total perspective, Rusiate now uses the first person plural possessive that implies a smaller group, *nodatou,* when he says *"sa nodatou na matanitu,"* "the government is ours." Now "we" or "us" is not a vast population including, impliedly, everybody worth considering, but rather it is a smaller, discrete number of "us" contrasted with a significant, roughly equal "them."

Taken as a whole, the debate is a contest not only between two cross-cousins anxious to perform well on a tape that can be played for others of their *yaqona* drinking friends later, but it is also a contest between two control communication systems. Tui manages to get possession of the modernist, *rarama* stance, and he tries to coopt the kinship/chiefly position by calling the Fiji Indians as "our relatives," *na wekada,* and he also refers to them as *turaga,* "gentlemen," implying a standing within the chiefly complex. But it is clear that the central argument—that leadership should be distributed on strictly rational grounds, with ability to lead measured only by academic accomplishment, goes to the heart of the modernist relationship system and is inconsistent with the patterns of authority distribution inherent in the private sphere of the kinship system or the public, civic realm constituted by the chiefly system.

As Rusiate begins to interpret the conflict situation from the perspective afforded by the discourse apparatus of the kinship/chiefly system, he abandons his initial support of education and "wisdom," *na vuku,* as a credential of leadership. Now, in fact he equates education with success in business and with the accumulation of money, which he portrays as dangerous to the indigenous Fijians. Using the exclusionary logic of the total system, he argues that *they* have education, *they* have money and success in business, *we* have only the land as an ultimate foundation as a people (A: 53-58). Reference to foundations, *yavu,* and permanence, *tudei* (A:52-53), is typical of traditional kinship/chiefly ritual language and impressive speech (Arno, 1985b).

But the critical question here is the connection between this kind of communication event and actions that may be taken in attempting to manage the conflict and change or maintain patterns of structural communication in the village and in the nation. Will these two men vote for the Alliance or for the Federation in the coming election? Will they or others engaged in similar discourse plan, participate in, or support a military coup aimed at removing a government perceived as too influenced by the Fiji Indians? Or would they reject such a coup and demand a return to pluralistic parliamentary government? My argument in this book has been that when an institutionalized control communication form of discourse takes root in the community and becomes dominant, it shapes the structural communication patterns of action in everyday life and makes them congruent with itself.

Although if one considers only the substance of the arguments that the two debaters make it seems like an even contest between the two forms of control discourse, the other, equally powerful dimension of conflict communication must also be taken into account. The form of the debate itself—the rules that govern who may speak to whom about what and what style—derives entirely from the kinship/chiefly control communication discourse. Tui and Rusiate are two cross-cousins engaged in a joking debate about conflict, and as such they are part of the larger social process of conflict talk described in detail in Chapter 5.

The present example perhaps gives a glimpse of the mechanism whereby a system of control communication operates as part of a society's formative context. The parties to the conflict talk episode can say almost whatever they want, but the way they say it and to whom they say it is strictly controlled. If the debate had included Epi, who is Tui's father and Rusiate's *vugona* (classificatory father-in-law), the modernist arguments based on a new calculus of social identities would have been reinforced because the parties would be acting out what they were advocating. But in fact, such a combination of debaters would have been out of the question on Yanuyanu.

Based on my direct observations and on what people told me about the rules of talk, I feel sure that if Epi had entered the house, the other two men would either have found some reason to leave or would have receded into the background while Epi carried out whatever business he had in mind. If he felt it necessary for some reason, Epi might have delivered a lecture on the coming election, but the contributions of the others would have been minimal.

My informants were well aware that the functioning of certain modern institutions requires that the traditional rules of talk be modified. Thus, I was assured that at a business meeting of the cooperative society, at a village-wide meeting with a government official, and in dealings with the police and courts, a man could, for example, speak up in front of his father-in-law or even contradict what his father or elder brother had said. But although they understood the logic of the communication patterns appropriate to these new fora, the villagers of Yanuyanu could not bring themselves to put it into practice. The grip of the dominant system was too tight.

I could never find even one example of the traditional rules' being violated in such situations, and in every case I knew about the opposite was true. At every such meeting the person whose presence would have made things awkward failed to show up, or people who could have spoken kept silent in the interests of decorum. Once, a young man was describing to a group of his cross-cousins a scene he had witnessed in which an elder man had made false claims to a government official about land boundaries. In telling about it, he cursed the old man and said that he was a liar who was just trying to gain more land for his own descent group. When I asked him if he had made any objection at the time, the young man assured me that that would not have been proper, given the age and status of the other man. But it was not necessary to say anything, he told me, because the man's lying would be punished by illness—either his own or that of his children or grandchildren.

Under circumstances like these, alternative communication systems can be known and talked about, but they cannot displace the dominant system. The more total it is, the more areas of life it regulates through its set of social identities and rules of communication, the more difficult it is to displace.

POWER AND PLEASURE

One aspect of the debate between Tui and Rusiate that does not come across in the bare transcript, but which the reader readily infers, is their enjoyment of participating in it. The psychic motor of the whole process of control communication is not social function but pleasure.[3] In other words, people do not engage in social control through talk because it is a necessary to public order but because it is a source of great pleasure.

Pleasure, then is part—perhaps a very important part—of a theory of conflict and communication. In conclusion, therefore, I will propose the outline of a theory of metaphor and discourse pleasure that derives from the formulation of the problem that I introduced in Chapter 2. In that model of language and communication, I posited three worlds, each defined by a distinct form of causation (Figure 2.1). Correspondingly, each is characterized by a specific form of pleasure and a mechanism of control associated with it.

Concentrating on, or giving theoretical primacy to, the outer world of physical reality, a materialist, realist perspective on conflict management would emphasize physical rewards and punishments. At this level, the relationship between pleasure and power is obvious. Pleasure is the reduction of tension or other uncomfortable state caused by an unsatisfied need. Providing or withholding the physical means of such reduction provides a powerful mechanism for imposing influence upon—exercising power over—another. Emphasizing this dimension of the total situation of conflict and control gives rise to approaches that assert that power grows from the barrel of a gun or from control of strategic resources. Certainly it is a part of the process that cannot be ignored, and examples of its use are abundant. In its 1990 secession struggle with Lithuania, therefore, the Soviet government employed, as one stage of imposing its will, the tactic of cutting off supplies of vital material resources and products. Just previously, the United States had been employing not only direct violence but also an

---

[3] In Chapter 5, I also described *madua*, shame, as a psychological force behind conflict management through talk. As a self-administered punishment of social origin, shame is and example of "unpleasure," as Freud called it. The pleasure of metaphor that I am referring to here is not strictly of social origin, in contrast.

economic embargo in order to bring down the Sandinista government in Nicaragua.

Clearly, however, the strictly materialist theory cannot account for all possible techniques of power because it recognizes—or gives absolute priority to—only one type of pleasure. Marx recognized that the usefulness of the physical object does not completely define its value in exchange because as a commodity it enters into a nonrealistic, socially constructed system of values. But while Marx interprets this transformation negatively, as part of the illusion generated by false ideology, a pragmatist like Peirce sees it as inevitable. For Peirce all knowledge of the real is indirect; we know things through ideas, and ideas are signs—representations that can never be identical with the object. Furthermore, signs are linked to one another, which creates the illusion that the objects themselves are so linked. In fact, they may not be, but those linkages seem to be an aspect of reality.

Objects of pleasure, therefore, are largely constructed through communication and are part of the social world. Bourdieu's (1984) work on fashion and taste illustrates the pervasive and obviously artificial realm within which people pursue objects or "looks" as if they were valuable but in which it is clear that such value is not based on a materialist usefulness. In the world of the social, just as in the outer world, the control of objects of pleasure is equated with power and therefore is at the heart of conflict and conflict management processes.

But this observation raises the question of whether power in the social realm is actually different from that of the real, outer world. One might argue that the communication system of the social world merely provides a way of distributing—through the construction of values, categories of analysis, and hierarchically linked social identities—power generated elsewhere. From such a perspective the only power constructed in the social world is itself a sign—a representation of a real object, and that object is the "real" power associated with the outer world.

The problem with two-world models of discourse is that they lend themselves to either of two kinds of reductionism. For some theorists, like Marx, the outer world of material reality is given priority, for others like Derrida, the social world of conventional signs is considered the more "real" of the two realities.

It is only by treating the third, inner world of the mind as distinct, however, that social causation—whose definition is necessary to social inquiry—can itself be understood as distinct. Social causation is different from natural causation in that it is a mediation, through the communication system of the group, between the inner and the outer regimes of causation, power, and pleasure.

Freud considered the primary process and its associated pleasure principle to be sharply distinct from the secondary process and its reality principle. In the *Interpretation of Dreams,* he portrays the primary process as attempting to reduce tension, thereby creating pleasure, by producing an image of the object associated in past experiences—through the medium of highly energized memory traces that record past pleasure—with the satisfaction of wants. The image, however, because it is not in fact the real object, fails to reduce the tension, or need. The reality principle develops in response to this problem and, recognizing the difference between the image and the real object, produces actual reduction of tension by employing whatever means necessary and possible to secure the real object. In serving the pleasure principle, the secondary process employs every sort of rational problem-solving technique in interaction with the outer and social worlds.

One of the necessary conditions required by the ego or secondary process in its work is the reduction of the intense level of psychic energy attached to memories so that strategic restraint—rather than impulsive, ineffective action—becomes possible. Memories and ideas need to be cooled off, in other words, so that they can be handled from an outer and social world perspective that insures a realistic, objective assessment of the prospects of pleasure. Freud suggests that this cooling takes places when the highly energized direct memories are converted into verbal memories. Language, therefore, is the essence of the secondary process and constitutes, as the symbolic interactionists also observed, the point of contact between the inner and the social worlds.

Viewed from the mechanical, anatomical perspective of Freud's model, the function posited for language fits very well with the idea, developed in semiotics, that signs are totally interconnected as elements in a system. This notion suggests a pathway—or an actual network of paths—along which psychic energy associated with the overly vivid and too stimulating nonverbal memory can be drained off and distributed in such a way that intensity is minimized and the considered, reasoned, and restrained pursuit of pleasure is possible.

But this mechanism also suggests the source of pleasure that is intrinsic to language itself, which is necessary to a nonreductionist account of social causation. If tension is represented by an uncomfortable buildup of psychic energy attached to a nonverbal memory, the reduction of that tension through the process of distribution over a field of verbal signs is not only the basis of realistic, objective reasoning but also a source of pleasure in and of itself. The outrushing flow of verbally fixed tension, expanding outward like a fluid escaping from a too-small container into a larger space, is experienced as pleasure, and it is a type of pleasure independent of the physical sphere. Going further with this idea, it seems plausible that psychic energy, once it enters the domain of language, is not in fact distributed in a totally flat pattern but adheres in clumps or may build up around certain semantic formations.

William Haas (1960, 1964) provides a useful model of this process when he argues that the semantic field of each word is ordered by a subjectively grasped but socially validated sense of normality. The verbal sign is related to others along two dimensions, the paradigmatic and the syntagmatic, but it is not related equally or in that same way to all members of the two sets. Rather, Haas argues, the semantic field formed by the two dimensions of contrast and association for each word is uniquely ordered by perceived comparative normality. The words immediately adjacent to the word being investigated in the paradigmatic dimension of its semantic field are those that frequently, easily, or normally can be substituted for it in a sentence or phrase. Thus "needle" would have a different cluster of closely adjacent paradigmatically related worlds than would "black." Similarly, syntagmatic clusters would be different also—that is, each would have a distinct set of phrases in which it would be likely to appear and in which it would not sound odd. Clearly Freud's technique of free association depends upon semantic formations in which the strength of association or contrast is intense at the core and tails off at the periphery.

From this Haasian perspective, relationships among near synonyms or antonyms can be understood as characteristic similarities or differences in the orderings of their respective semantic fields. Most important, this relational way of looking at meaning provides an interpretation of metaphor, which is the key concept in any discussion of verbal art and verbal pleasure. A metaphor presents itself to the mind as an overlapping of the semantic fields of two signs that are normally considered remote from one another.[4] The metaphor "works" to the extent that the two fields, from the unique perspective provided by the context of the metaphor's use in a specific instance, are experienced as coinciding. The further the ripples of the metaphor spread—the more extensive the area of unlikely and unanticipated similarities becomes as the comparison expands from its core—the more profound the metaphor and the greater the pleasure it provides.

---

[4] It is obvious that the semantic fields of two words that are remote from one another or "unrelated" have quite a different relationship from that between two words that are antonyms. Antonyms are very closely related and share a good bit of the core areas of their fields. They are arranged, however, in such a way that certain central (that is, frequent or normal) syntagmatic settings of one of the pair would be extremely abnormal for the other.

Combining a Haassian theory of metaphor with a Freudian theory of pleasure and the dynamics of psychic tension yields the outline of a theory of discourse pleasure and points the way toward a more complete explanation of the role of talk in conflict management. A metaphor is capable of exerting its own distinct form of power over the individual, commanding his or her attention and inducing an active exploration of asserted patterns of interconnectedness among signs by providing pleasure. The amount of pleasure, and the corresponding power of the metaphor, is related to the amount of psychic tension adhering to the primary leg of the metaphor and also to the quality of the metaphor—its unexpectedness and the scope of linkage it suggests between the two terms. The suddenness and the degree of tension reduction involved in the specific metaphor determines its pleasure potential and its power.

Obviously metaphor cannot be explained at the level of the word or the pair of words that it links. Looking at the meaning of the words as fields, uniquely configured by patterns of usage at the sentence level, shows that metaphor depends on a total system of interconnected words arranged in relatively distinct clusters (see Kittay, 1987). At the same time, the notion of normality of use implies that more than just words are involved in metaphor. The nonlanguage situation of use also defines the process of metaphor, and signs other than words—shapes, colors, sounds, textures, and so on—that have meanings built of systematic relationships of association and contrast with one another also have the potential for artistic pleasure, and the consequent power to motivate behavior, inherent in metaphor.

At a larger level, that of broader units of discourse, the same process of metaphor provides an internal source of pleasure and power, and it is at this level that control communication operates as a mechanism of social control. Here the units of the metaphor are events, represented in narrative, and the other events related to them sytagmatically and paradigmatically in dimensions of association and contrast constitute fields of discourse meaning that can be linked in discrete forms of conflict discourse—control communication institutions. Within these systems, seen as ordered fields of meaning, the relationships of contrast and association among units of social action, represented in narrative as events, are created through habitual action and reflective codification in the process of conflict management. Thus event A is given meaning paradigmatically in terms of similarity and contrast with events B, C, and D. In the syntagmatic dimension, the sequential relationships in which A follows X or Y and precedes W or Z represent statements of communicative causation.

For example, the military coup of May 1987 was an event that quickly became a unit of narrative discourse throughout the country, the region, and beyond. It was an event of considerable news value in that it posed a serious potential threat to the interests of a wide range of readers (Arno, 1984). As narrative, therefore, the event became invested with a great deal of tension. A violent, highly irregular change of government in a peaceful country immediately brings into question every citizen's government-protected interests, which include physical safety, property rights, currency value, and social status. As noted above, discourse-centered institutions from the mass media to village *yaqona* sessions wasted no time in placing the event into control communication perspectives, and in doing so they were drawing upon metaphor as a source of power to be used in dealing with the problems the event posed.

A control communication system, as a semantic field with well developed pathways in directions of contrast and association, allows the tension associated with the event to flow off into a wider distribution so that the event can be dealt with cooly and rationally rather than emotionally and impulsively. Thus the coup can be thrust by discourse into frameworks of meaning that vary from Marxism to fundamentalist Christianity, or from liberalism to kinship/chiefly traditionalism. If a control communication system can draw effectively enough upon the discourse pleasure it provides, which depends upon language or language-like processes of metaphor, it can exert power from the social source represented by the communication system of roles and behavioral expectations it is able to establish and maintain in everyday life.

CONCLUSIONS

In this book I have posed a set of theoretical objectives and a set of ethnographic ones. In terms of theoretical development, I have sought a linkage between the two traditions in discourse analysis, the micro tradition that focuses on conversation, and the macro tradition that deals with societal discourse formations. In doing so, I have abandoned the "two world" approach, characteristic of ideal/real or idea/object theories such as Saussure's definition of the sign, and adopted a "three world" view which is more consistent with pragmatism. Peirce's view of the sign as a set of relationships among object, sign, and interpretant, for example, corresponds roughly to the outer, social, and inner worlds I have discussed. In my view, a world is defined by a distinct form of causation, and communicative causation is associated with the social world. In every community a language system links the social and the inner worlds and governs the inner, while a communication system links the social and outer worlds and governs the social.

In this theoretical setting, conflict management assumes paramount importance in the social world, generating through its operations the communication system and the regime of communicative causation specific to the community. Conflict management is seen as a form of discourse that cycles between problems of truth and power and between modes of language and communication. Finally I deal with the linkages between talk, conflict, power, and pleasure. By assuming two distinct sources of power that are drawn upon in the social world, one based in the outer and the other in the inner world, I avoid the reductionisms that two-world conflict theories tend toward. A regime of communicative causation, therefore, and the communication system that it grows out of and creates simultaneously, is in every distinct social context a unique synthesis of the characteristics of the inner and outer worlds.

This theoretical point emphasizes the ethnographic imperative in conflict studies, and my ethnographic objectives in the book have been to describe the talk about conflict that takes place on an island in Fiji's Southern Lau Group. Rules of communication that governs message flow among relatives and among the hierarchically ranked groups that constitute the political structure of the island provide a framework within which messages embodied as precisely calculated movements of food, useful and ceremonial goods, and ritual performances of speeches, music, and dance move back and forth among individuals and groups. These messages are a structural conversation of statements and counterstatements that expresses the political economy as well as the artistic life of the community.

Conflict management on Yanuyanu is carried out through a combination of the building blocks of the communication system—social identities, the rules for message flow among them, and the types of recognized communication events that make up the discourse economy of the community. Looking at conflict management in this way requires a redefinition of the case and the case method in legal anthropology. A case is a set of conversations about conflict that are dispersed in time and space and to which no one person can have complete access. The ethnographer, like the villager, can only hope to intersect a sample of the communication events that constitute the case. Interpreting them requires an investigation of the communication system and the institutions of control communication that are operative in the community with respect to particular types of conflict (Merry, 1990; Conley & O'Barr, 1990).

As many ethnographers who have had the good fortune to work in Fiji have noted, the Fijians tend to be a people of highly developed verbal and social skills. Their rather exquisite sensibilities in this arena of life lead one to the realization that much of their world is talk. In their cultural emphasis on the power and pleasure of talk, the villagers of Yanuyanu delineate a dimension of social life that has application everywhere, and not least among the community of social analysts whose work itself constitutes an attempt to build an instrument of control communication but which may or may not be a source of pleasure.

Appendix A: Political Debate Recorded on Yanuyanu in 1971
(..... = pause, [   ] = inaudible)

1. TUI: Rusiate, a cava ko nanuma ni.....kevaka sa na mani
   Rusiate, what do you think about.....if this election
2. vakayacori na veidigidigi oqo sa ra winitaka na kai
   finally takes place [and] the Indians win...
3. Idia.....a cava beka o nanuma e na yaco e Viti e na
   what might you think would happen in Fiji in
4. gauna mai muri?
   the future?
5. RUSIATE: Io...ko i au...baleta ni kevaka e na me yaco
   Yes...I...because if the election takes
6. na veidigidigi...ko i au, au dau nuitaki ira tale ga na
   place.....I, I am disposed to place my confidence also in
7. turaga ni Idia baleta ni ira turaga vuku. Sa le' levu
   the gentlemen of India because they are wise [educated]
8. vei ira 'lawya', ka le' levu vci ira.....vata kei
   gentlemen. Many of them are lawyers, and many of them...
9. iratou na mata...e le' levu na tamata vakoroi.
   together with their representatives [in parliament]...many are
   persons with degrees.
10. Mai vei iratou.....au nanuma e lewe levu cake mai vei
    Compared with them.....I think many more than...

11. .....ki vei iratou na noda mata i taukei. Oya na ka
than our representatives of the taukei. This is

12. au nanuma ni na rairai uasivi cake tale ga kina me
the thing I think appears excellent again in that

13. iratou taura na veiliutaki. Ia, e dua na ka au
they take their leadership. Well, one thing that I

14. taqayataka vakalevu.....A cava na nanuma, Tui,
worry a lot about.....What do you think, Tui,

15. kevaka iratou sa na mai winitaka na veidigidigi m'eratou
if they do win the election so that they

16. veiliutaki, e na sega ni dua na ka e na.....e ratou
assume leadership, isn't there something....

17. vakatubulega kina e na noda vanua ogo e Viti?
they
will cause trouble about in our nation here of Fiji?

18. Se a cava na nomu i nanuma kina, Tui?
or what is your thought about it, Tui?

19. TUI: Au vakabauta ni.....ni'u dua vata tale ga e na
I think that.....that I am also in accord with

20. nomu vakasama. Au vakabauta ni na rairai.....sega ni
your thinking. I think that it will appear.....it will

21. dua na ka.....e na uasivi tale ga, kevaka e ra na
not be anything...it will also be excellent, if they will

22. veiliutaki na.....na wekada na Idia e na noda matanitu
lead, the.....our kinsmen the Indians in our nation

23. oqo ko Viti. Au kila ni.....ni da sa dua vata.....' da
here, Fiji. I know that.....that we are in accord...that

24. sa veikilai tovo. E na rairai tautauvata ga e na gauna
we know one another's cultures. It will appear just the same as in
the time

25. ni noda veiliutaki e yaco tiko e na gauna oqo. Se e dua
of our leadership that is happening at present. And

26. tale na ka au nanuma e na ka e baleti Viti...kevaka e ra
another thing I think in the matter of Fiji...if they

27. na veiliutaki tale e so na mataqali tamata.....Idia, se
were to lead, some other races of people...Indians, or

28. Vavalagi, se Taina, ko i au nanuma, noqu nanuma taucoko
Europeans, or Chinese, I think, my complete belief is,

29. ni na uasivi cake. E na tautauvata kevaka ga e ra sa
that it will be wonderful. It will be just the same if

30. vuli vinaka, me levu na koroi ni vuli e ra rawata.
    only they are well educated, with many academic degrees that they
    have earned.
31. Se ra vakaciciva kina nodra koroi. Se au vinakata
    or they are pursuing their degrees. Or I wish to
32. kevaka e so tale na vakasama ko nanuma?
    know if you have some other thoughts?
33. RUSIATE: O, io. Ko i au na...e dina ni au a kaya vata
    Oh, yes. I will...it's true that I spoke
34. kei na nomu vosa ni na...Dina ni sa vuli vinaka tale
    consistently with what you said.....In truth, you are
35. ga ko iko.....e kei sa laki via.....sa vaka me laki
    well educated yourself.....here it sort of goes...it's as if it becomes
36. duidui tale na [voli] ni nodaru vakasama...baleta e dua
    different again the [spin] of our thinking because this is
37. na mataqali oqo...e da kila tu kedra talanoa me dua na
    a race here...we well know their reputation as a
38. mataqali vunitaka lo tu na nodra ka e tauba' tiko
    race that hides what they keep defensively fortified
39. e lomadra. Ia, na ka au taqayataka tale ga...sa...
    in side themselves. Well, the thing I worry about also...
40. era mani tubuleqa e mai na gauna sara e ra taura
    is...they wil finally cause trouble as soon as they
41. rawa kina na veiliutaki. E ra taura na veiliutaki
    are able to take the leadership. They take the
42. ...e ra na mani veisautaka na...na lewa ni noda
    leadership...they will finally change the...the law of
43. matabose ni qele maroroi. Mai kea sa na vakarerevaki
    our [native] lands trust commission. This will be very
44. sara kina kevaka e ratou mani taura na veiliutaki.
    frightening if they finally obtain the leadership.
45. Veitalia mada na nodratou vuku.....m'eratou na
    Nevermind, if you please, their wisdom...that they will
46. veiliuitaki vinaka kina. E sa dua na ka va'rerevaki
    govern so nicely with. It's a very frightening thing
47. sara vei keda na i taukei. Oya, me eratou veisautaka
    to us taukei. Right there, that they change
48. na lewa ni noda qele, me vaka e da sa rairai tu e na
    the law of our land, that we are seeing right

49. gauna oqo na kena vinaka, Tui. Sega ni [ ]
    now the benefits of, Tui. Our land cannot

50. vei keda noda qele. Sa tu na kena lewa me
    [ ] among us. The law is established to

51. taqomaki kina na qele maroroi nei taukei. Au nanuma
    protect the entrusted land of the taukei. I think

52. ni sai koya na.....e dua na yavu dei.....sai otioti
    that this is.....a firm foundation...it is

53. beka ni ka meda deitoki nei taukei. E da sega ni
    perhaps the last thing that anchors us taukei. We are

54. rawata vakalevu na i lavo me vakataki ira, me ira
    not able to make a lot of money like they do, so they

55. sa vuli vinaka. Nodra veibisinisi lelevu sa tubu
    can be well educated. Their many large businesses flourish

56. oqori me baleta tiko na nodra sa vuli vinaka. Ia,
    here because they are so well educated. Well,

57. e ra sa rawata vakalevu mai kina na i lavo.
    they are able to obtain lots of money from it.

58. Ia, sa qai vo vaka...sa qai vo ga na otioti ni ka e da
    Well, there then remains like...there then remains only the
    ultimate thing we

59. vakanuinuitaka kina, oya na qele e da sa mai tawana
    place our hopes in, that is the land that we occupy here

60. vata oqo ka sa tiko e ligada i taukei.
    together that is in the hands of the taukei.

61. E vakacava ke iratou sa mani veiliutaki? E sa mani
    And what if they finally take the leadership? Then

62. nodratou tale ga na lewa ni kena vuki. A cava ko
    their's also will be the power of its reversal. What

63. nanuma kina, Tui?
    do you think about it, Tui?

64. TUI: Io. Noqu nanuma e kea ni...au vakabauta ni kevaka
    Yes. My thinking here about...I think that if

65. era sa na veiliutaki na Idia, e na sega tale ga ni rawa
    the Indians come to power, we will never again be able

66. ni da na tarova na nodra lewa na noda matanitu. Au
    to stop their control of our government. I

67. vakabauta ni ka taucoko tukuna oqori sa na...sa ra na
    think that everything talked about here will...the

68. vakayacora ga na Idia. E na sega ni rawa ni tarova
Indians will bring about. It cannot be prevented

69. kevaka e ra sa na winitaka na veidigidigi oqo. Sa
if they win this election.

70. vaka evei?
what about that?

71. RUSIATE: Oya duadua sara ga na ka au [   ] vakabitaka sai
That is the most important thing that I [   ] emphasize

72. koya sara na ka...me baleta noda qele...
that indeed is the ting...concerning our land...

73. TUI: E na qai.....e vakacava ni...au vakabauta ni sa sega
But then...what if...I think that there is nothing

74. soti ni taqayataki ni sa tu na...ni sa e ra na wini...
much to worry about if there remains...if they do win...

75. e na tiko tale ga na noda matapati, ka e ra na saqa tiko
our party will be there too, and they will be pushing

76. ...e ra na veisaqa tiko e na ganna tiko ni veiliutaki oya.
...they will be opposing during that period of leadership.

77. Au vakabauta ni na sega soti ni dua na kena taqayataki
I think there is nothing much to worry about

78. bera na mani kaukauwa ni noda matapati nei taukei
before our party of the taukei will be powerful

79. ka na vakavuna me cicitaki vinaka ga kina na matanitu
and that will cause the government to be run correctly.

80. Se e dua na vanua eratou na drusa rawa kina kevaka e
That is one place they can be beaten in if they

81. ratou na via tamabokoca na matanitu i taukei. Au
wish to destroy the government of the taukei. I

82. vakabauta ni sega ni dua na ka kevaka e ra veiliutaki.
think it will be no problem if they lead.

83. RUSIATE: O...e kei e duidui kin a vakalevu nodaru vakasama.
Oh...here our thoughts are very much different.

84. Oqo sa na...E ratou sa na taura kina na veiliutaki
Here it will...They will take the leadership

85. e noda vanua oqo. E sa na ca sara tale ga na noda
in our country here. This will damage badly also our

86. tauri tiko oqo na...na "Alliance Pati", noda liuliu tiko
controlling here the...the Alliance Party, our leader here

87. oqo na gone turaga Ratu Mara.....Me keia...sa tu kina na
the noble gentleman Ratu Mara.....Here...is where the

88. kaukauwa e na liga ni matanitu.....Sa nodatou na
    strength is in the arm of the government.....The

89. matanitu. Sa rawa datou vakatulewa e na matanitu
    government is ours. We are able to control the

90. e na ka me vakyacori. E dina, na tabana ni veisaqa...
    government in the things it does. In truth, the side of
    counterforce...

91. na "oposition pati"...sa dau kena i vakarau ga...
    the opposition party...its only role...

92. e [vakadi'lawya'?].....se me vakaliutaka tiko mai na
    is to [   ].....or to be led forth

93. na veika sa nanuma na matanitu me vakayacori. E sa na
    in whatever the government decides will be done. Truly,

94. vakayacori e dina ga.....E kena i vakarau ga e na veimatanitu
    it will be done.....The only role in each government

95. "vakaopisitionpati" me ra dau vakaliutaka mada na veika
    of the opposition party is that they are led in everything

96. vakacava. O ya na ka au [   ] kina me taqayataki
    whatever. This is the reason I [   ] in to worry

97. meratou taura na veiliutaki e kei me baleta noda qele.
    that they take leadership here because of our land.

98. Au nanuma ni rairai sa rauta toka mada ga, Tui,
    I think that looks like about enough perhaps, Tui,

99. nodaru veivosaki nikua. Sa vakacava Misita Adriu?
    of our discussion today. What about it, Mr. Andrew?

100. Vinaka vakalevu na nomu solia donu me keirau veivosaki
     Thanks very much for giving permission for our discussion

101. ...me baleti na ka oqo, Misita Adriu, vinaka vakalevu.
     ...about this thing, Mr. Andrew, thank you very much.

References

Althusser, L., & Balibar, E. (1979). *Reading capital.* New York: Shocken Books.

Arno, A. (1974). *Conflict management in a Fijian village.* Doctoral thesis, Harvard University, Cambridge, MA.

Arno, A. (1976a). Joking, avoidance, and authority: Verbal performance as an object of exchange in Fiji. *Journal of the Polynesian Society, 85*(1), 71–86.

Arno, A. (1976b). Ritual reconciliation and village conflict management in Fiji. *Oceania, XLVII*(1), 49–65.

Arno, A. (1979a). Conflict, ritual, and social structure on Yanuyanu Island, Fiji. *Bijdragen, 153,* 1–17.

Arno, A. (1979b). A grammar of conflict: Informal procedure on an island in Lau, Fiji. In K.-F Koch (Ed.), *Patterns of conflict management: Comparative studies in the anthropology of law* (Vol. 4, pp. 41–68). Boston: Sijthoff and Noordhoff.

Arno, A. (1980). Fijian gossip as adjudication: A communication model of social control. *Journal of Anthropological Research, 36*(3), 343–360.

Arno, A. (1984). Conflict, communication, and storyline: The news media as actors in cultural context. In A. Arno & W. Dissanayake (Eds.), *The news media in national and international conflict* (pp. 1–15). Boulder, CO: Westview.

Arno, A. (1985a). Structural communication and control communication: An interactionist perspective on legal and customary procedures for conflict management. *American Anthropologist, 87*(1), 40–55.

Arno, A. (1985b). Impressive speeches and persuasive talk: Traditional patterns of political communication from the perspective of Pacific ideal types. *Oceania, LVI*(2), 124–137.

Arno, A. (1990). Disentangling indirectly: The joking debate in Fijian social control. In K. Watson-Gegeo & G. White (Eds.), *Disentangling: Conflict discourse in Pacific societies.* Stanford: Stanford University Press.

Arno, A. (1980). Fijian gossip as adjudication: A communication model of social control. *Journal of Anthropological Research, 36*(3), 343–360.

Arno, A. (1984). Conflict, communication, and storyline: The news media as actors in cultural context. In A. Arno & W. Dissanayake (Eds.), *The news media in national and international conflict* (pp. 1–15). Boulder, CO: Westview.

Arno, A. (1985a). Structural communication and control communication: An interactionist perspective on legal and customary procedures for conflict management. *American Anthropologist, 87*(1), 40–55.

Arno, A. (1985b). Impressive speeches and persuasive talk: Traditional patterns of political communication from the perspective of Pacific ideal types. *Oceania, LVI*(2), 124–137.

Arno, A. (1990). Disentangling indirectly: The joking debate in Fijian social control. In K. Watson-Gegeo & G. White (Eds.), *Disentangling: Conflict discourse in Pacific societies*. Stanford: Stanford University Press.

Austin, J.L. (1962). *How to do things with words*. Oxford: University of Oxford Press.

Austin, J. (1861). *The province of jurisprudence determined* (2nd ed.). London: J. Murray.

Barton, R.F. (1919). *Ifugao law* (Vol. 15, No. 1, and 1969). Berkeley: University of California Press.

Barton, R.F. (1963). *Philippine pagans: The autobiographies of three Ifugaos*. Hyde Park: University Books. (Original work published 1938)

Benveniste, E. (1971). *Problems in general linguistics*. Coral Gables: University of Miami Press.

von Bertalanffy, L. (1968). *General systems theory: Foundations, development, applications* (rev. ed.). New York: George Braziller.

Bernstein, B. (1971). *Class, codes, and control*. London: Routledge and Kegan Paul.

Bilmes, J. (1986). *Discourse and behavior*. New York: Plenum Press.

Bohannon, P. (1957). *Justice and judgement among the Tiv of Nigeria*. London: Oxford University Press.

Borofsky, R. (1987). *Making history: Pukapukans and anthropological constructions of knowledge*. New York: Cambridge University Press.

Bourdieu, P. (1984). *Distinction: A social critique of the judgement of taste* (trans. R. Nice). Cambridge, MA: Harvard University Press.

Brenneis, D.L. (1973). *Conflict and communication in a Fijian Indian community*. Doctoral thesis, Harvard University, Cambridge, MA.

Brenneis, D.L. (1988). Language and disputing. *Annual Reviews in Anthropology, 17,* 221–237.

Brenneis, D.L., & Meyers, F.R. (1984). *Dangerous words: Language and politics in the Pacific*. New York: New York University Press.

Burt, E.A. (1932). *The metaphysical foundations of modern science* (rev. ed.). Garden City, NY: Doubleday and Company.

Conley, J.M., & O'Barr, W.M. (1990). *Rules versus relationships: The ethnography of legal discourse*. Chicago: University of Chicago Press.

Coupland, N. (1988). Introduction: Towards a stylistics of discourse. In N. Coupland (Ed.), *Styles of discourse*. New York: Croom Helm.

Danzig, R. (1973). Toward the creation of a complementary, decentralized system of criminal justice. *Stanford Law Review, 26*(1).

Davidson, L.E., Rosenberg, M.L., Mercy, J.A., Franklin, J., & Simmons, J.T. (1989). An epidemiologic study of risk factors in two teenage suicide clusters. *Journal of the American Medical Association, 262*(19), 2687–2692.

Dean, E., & Ritova, A. (1988). *Rabuka: No other way*. Suva, Fiji: The Marketing Team International, Ltd.

Derrida, J. (1978). *Writing and difference* (trans. A. Bass). Chicago: University of Chicago Press.

Epstein, A.L. (1967). The case method in the field of law. In A.L. Epstein (Ed.), *The craft of social anthropology* (pp. 205–230). New York: Travistock.

Epstein, A.L. (1974). Introduction. In A.L. Epstein (Ed.), *Contention and dispute Aspects of law and social control in Melanesia* (p. 1–39). Canberra, Australia: ANU.

Favret-Saada, J. (1980). *Deadly words: Witchcraft in the Bocage*. New York: Cambridge University Press.

Foucault, M. (1965). *Madness and civilization: A history of insanity in the age of reason*. New York: Pantheon.

Foucault, M. (1972). *The archaeology of knowledge* (trans. A.M. Sheridan Smith). London: Travistock.

Foucault, M. (1977). *Discipline and punishment*. London: Allen Lane.

Foucault, M. (1981). The order of discourse. In R. Young (Ed.), *Untying the text: A post structuralist reader*. Boston: Routledge and Kegan Paul.

France, P. (1969). *The charter of the land: Custom and colonization in Fiji*. New York: Oxford University Press.

Frankl, V.E. (1963). *Man's search for meaning: An introduction to logotherapy*. New York: Washington Square Press.

Freud, S. (1953). *the interpretation of dreams. Vol. IV-V. The standard edition of the complete psychological works of Sigmund Freud*. London: The Hogarth Press.

Garrett, J. (1990). Uncertain sequel: The social and religious scene in Fiji since the coups. *The Contemporary Pacific, 2*(1), 87–111. *Journal of Communication, 35*(1), 76–88.

Gibbs, J.L., Jr. (1963). The Kpelle moot: A therapeutic model for the informal settlement of disputes. *Africa, 33*, 1–11.

Giddens, A. (1976). *New rules of sociological method*. New York: Basic Books.

Giddens, A. (1979). *Central problems in social theory*. Cambridge: University of Cambridge Press.

Gluckman, M. (1955). *The judicial process among the Barotse of Northern Rhodesia*. Manchester: Manchester University Press.

Gluckman, M. (1965). *The ideas in Barotse jurisprudence*. New Haven, CT: Yale University Press.

Glucksman, M. (1974). *Structuralist analysis in contemporary social thought: A comparison of the theories of Claude Levi-Strauss and Louis Althusser.* Boston: Routledge and Kegan Paul.

Goldman, L.R. (1983). *Talk never dies: The language of Huli disputes.* New York: Travistock.

Gould, M.S., & Shaffer, D. (1986). The impact of suicide in television movies. *New England Journal of Medicine, 315*(11), 690–694.

Gouldner, A.W. (1970). *The coming crisis of Western sociology.* New York: Basic Books.

Greenhouse, C.J. (1986). *Praying for justice.* Ithaca, NY: Cornell University Press.

Grice, H.P. (1975). Logic and conversation. In P. Cole & J.L. Morgan (Eds.), *Syntax and semantics, vol. 3, speech acts.* New York: Academic Press.

Groves, M. (1963). The nature of Fijian society. *Journal of the Polynesian Society, 72,* 272.

Gulliver, P.H. (1963). *Social control in an African society.* Boston: Boston University Press.

Gulliver, P.H. (1969). Case studies of law in non-western societies. In L. Nader (Ed.), *Law in culture and society.* Chicago: Aldine.

Gulliver, P.H. (1971). *Neighbors and networks: The idiom of kinship in social action among the Ndendeuli of Tanzania.* Berkeley: University of California Press.

Gumperz, J.J. (1982). *Language and social identity.* New York: Cambridge University Press.

Haas, W. (1960). Linguistic structures. *Word, 16,* 251–276.

Haas, W. (1964). Semantic value. *Proceedings of the Ninth International Congress of Linguistics* (Cambridge, MA, 1962). The Hague: Mouton.

Habermas, J. (1979). What is universal pragmatics? In *Communication and the evolution of society* (pp. 1–68). Boston: Beacon Press.

Habermas, J. (1984). *The theory of communicative action.* Boston: Beacon Press.

Hanley, R. (1987, March 12). 4 Jersey teen-agers kill themselves in death pact. *New York Times,* p. A1.

Hart, H.L.A. (1961). *The concept of law.* Oxford: Clarendon Books.

Hart, H.M., Jr., & Sacks, A.M. (1958). *The legal process: Basic problems in the making and application of law* (tent. ed.). Cambridge, MA: Harvard University Press.

Hawkings, S.T. (1988). *A brief history of time.* New York: Bantam Books.

Heidegger, M. (1962). The question concerning technology. In W. Lovitt (trans.), *The question concerning technology and other essays.* New York: Harper and Row.

Hickson, L. (1975). *The i Soro: Ritual apology and avoidance of punishment in Fijian dispute settlement.* Doctoral thesis, Harvard University, Cambridge, MA.

Hocart, A.M. (1929). *Lau Islands, Fiji* (Bernice P. Bishop Museum Bulletin, No. 62). Honolulu: Bishop Museum.

Hudson, W.H. (1921). *A traveller in little things.* New York: Dutton.

Hume, D. (1969). *A treatise of human nature.* New York: Penguin Books. (Original work published 1739)

Hunt, A. (1982). Dichotomy and contradiction in the sociology of law. In P. Beirne & R. Quinney (Eds.), *Marxism and law.* New York: Wiley.

Hymes, D. (1986). Discourse: Scope without depth. *International Journal of the Sociology of Language, 57,* 49–89.

Innes, H. (1951). *The bias of communication.* Toronto: University of Toronto Press.

Innes, H. (1972). *Empire and communications.* Toronto: University of Toronto Press.

Jakobson, R. (1960). Linguistics and poetics. In T.A. Sebeok (Ed.), *Style in language.* Cambridge: MIT Press.

Kaplan, M. (1990). Meaning, agency, and colonial history: Navosavakadua and the *Tuka* movement in Fiji. *American Ethnologist, 17*(1), 3–22.

Kelsen, H. (1943). *Society and nature.* Chicago: University of Chicago Press.

Kelsen, H. (1967). *Pure theory of law* (trans. M. Knight). Berkeley: University of California Press.

Kittay, E.F. (1987). *Metaphor: Its cognitive force and linguistic structure.* New York: Oxford University Press.

Koch, K.-F. (1974). *War and peace in Jalemo.* Cambridge: Harvard University Press.

Labov, W. (1973). *Language in the inner city: Studies in the Black English vernacular.* Philadelphia: University of Pennsylvania Press.

Lal, B.V., & Peacock, K.M. (1990). Researching the Fiji coups. *The Contemporary Pacific, 2*(1), 183–195.

Lasswell, H. (1948). The structure and function of communication in society. In L. Bryson (Ed.), *The communication of ideas.* New York: Institute for Religious and Social Studies.

Leach, E. (1961). *Pul Ileya, a village in Ceylon: A study of land tenure and kinship.* Cambridge: University Press.

Llewellyn, K., & Hoebel, E.A. (1941). *The Cheyenne way.* Norman: The University of Oklahoma Press.

Macdonald, B. (1990). The literature of the Fiji coups. *The Contemporary Pacific, 2*(1), 198–207.

Malinowski, B. (1923). The problem of meaning in primitive languages. In C.K. Ogden & I.A. Richards (Eds.), *The meaning of meaning* (Supp. I). New York: Harcourt, Brace and World.

Malinowski, B. (1926). *Crime and custom in savage society.* New York: Harcourt Brace.

Marcus, G.E., & Fischer, M.M.J. (1986). *Anthropology as cultural critique: An experimental moment in the human sciences.* Chicago: University of Chicago Press.

Marx, K., & Engels, F. (1947). *The German ideology.* New York: International Publishers.

MacCormick, N. (1981). *H.L.A. Hart.* Stanford: Stanford University Press.

McIver, R.M. (1942). *Social causation.* New York: Ginn and Company.

Merry, S.E. (1982). The social organization of mediation in nonindustrial societies: Implications for informal justice in America. In R. Abel (Ed.), *The politics of informal justice, Vol. 2, comparative studies.* New York: Academic Press.

Merry, S.E. (1990). *Getting justice and getting even: Legal consciousness among working-class Americans.* Chicago: University of Chicago Press.

Moerman, M. (1988). *Talking culture: Ethnography and conversation analysis.* Philadelphia: University of Pennsylvania Press.

Moore, S.F. (1978). *Law as process: An anthropological approach.* Boston: Routledge and Kegan Paul.

Nader, L. (1965). The anthropological study of law. *American Anthropologist, 67*(6), 3–32.

New York Times. (1978a, March 14). 2 Illinois youths commit suicide. Page A30.

New York Times. (1987b, March 17). Illinois boy, 14, a suicide. Page B2.

O'Barr, W.M. (1981). *Linguistic evidence: Language, power, and strategy in the courtroom.* New York: Academic Press.

O'Barr, W.M., & Conley, J.M. (1985). Litigant satisfaction versus legal adequacy in small claims court narratives. *Law and Society Review, 19*(4), 661–701.

Oliver, D.L. (1955). *A Solomon Island society: Kinship and leadership among the Siuai of Bougainville.* Boston: Beacon Press.

Ochs, E. (1988). *Culture and language development: Language acquisition and language socialization in a Samoan village.* New York: Cambridge University Press.

Peirce, C.S. (1955). Pragmatism in retrospect, a last formulation. In J. Buchler (Ed.), *Philosophical writings of Peirce.* New York: Dover.

Phillips, D.P., & Carstensen, L.L. (1986). Clustering of teenage suicides after television news stories about suicide. *New England Journal of Medicine, 315*(11), 685–689.

Phillips, D.P., & Paight, D.J. (1987). The impact of televised movies about suicide: A replicative study. *New England Journal of Medicine, 317*(13), 809–811.

Pike, K.L. (1967). *Language in relation to a unified theory of the structure of human behavior.* The Hague: Mouton.

Pospisil, L. (1971). *Anthropology of law: A comparative theory.* New York: Harper and Row.

Pound, R. (1942). *Social control through law.* New Haven, CT: Yale University Press.

Pound, R. (1959). *Jurisprudence.* St. Paul, MN: Westview.

Quain, B. (1948). *Fijian village: An anthropological account of Fijian institutions, ethics, and personalities.* Chicago: University of Chicago Press.

Rothfeld, C. (1988). What do law schools teach? Almost anything. *New York Times,* p. B8.

Russell, B. (1943). *A history of Western philosophy: And its connection with political and social circumstances from the earliest times to the present.* New York: Simon and Schuster.

Ryle, G. (1949). *The concept of mind.* London, Hutchinson: University Library.

Sacks, H., Schegloff, E., & Jefferson, G. (1974). A simplist systematics for the organization of turn taking for conversation. *Language, 50*(4), 196–235.

Sahlins, M.D. (1962). *Moala: Culture and nature on a Fijian island.* Ann Arbor, MI: University of Michigan Press.

Sahlins, M.D. (1985). *Islands of history.* Chicago: University of Chicago Press.

Saussure, F. (1966). *Course in general linguistics.* New York: McGraw-Hill.

Schegloff, E., Jefferson, G., & Sacks, H. (1977). The preference for self-correction in the organization of repair in conversation. *Language, 53,* 361–382.

Searle, J.R. (1976). The classification of illocutionary acts. *Language in Society, 5,* 1–24.

Smith, A. (1978). *Lectures on jurisprudence: Report dated 1766* (R.L. Meak, D.D. Raphael, & P.G. Stein, eds.). Oxford: Clarendon Press.

Starr, J., & Collier, J.F. (Eds.). (1989). *History and power in the study of law.* Ithaca: Cornell University Press.

Thompson, L. (1940). *Southern Lau, Fiji: An ethnography* (Bernice P. Bishop Museum Bulletin No. 162). Honolulu: Bishop Museum.

Turner, J.W. (1987). Blessed to give and to receive: Ceremonial exchange in Fiji. *Ethnology, XXVI*(3), 209.

Unger, R.M. (1986). *The critical legal studies movement.* Cambridge, MA: Harvard Law School.

Unger, R.M. (1988). *False necessity: Anti-necessitarian social theory in the service of radical democracy.* New York: Cambridge University Press.

Van Velsen, J. (1967). The extended-case method and situational analysis. In A.L. Epstein (Ed.), *The craft of social anthropology.* New York: Travistock.

Vinogradoff, P. (1920). *Outline of historical jurisprudence.* London: Oxford University Press.

Watson-Gegeo, K., & White, G.M. (Eds.). (1990). *Disentangling: Conflict discourse in Pacific societies.* Stanford: Stanford University Press.

Wittgenstein, L. (1954). *The blue and brown books.* New York: Macmillan.

Wittgenstein, L. (1967). *Philosophical investigations.* London, Oxford: Basil Blackwell.

Wittgenstein, L. (1979). *Notebooks, 1914–1916* (2nd ed., G.H. Von Wright & G.E.M. Anscombe, eds.). Chicago: University of Chicago Press.

Yngvesson, B. (1978). The Atlantic fishermen. In L. Nader & M. Todd, Jr. (Eds.), *The disputing process: Law in ten societies.* New York: Columbia University Press.

Author Index

Subject Index

A

Authority, defined as communication pattern, 68, 70, 87

Avoidance, communication pattern among relatives, 68–69

B

Barriers to communication, 38–39

Batinilovo, *see* i tokatoka

Bosenivanua, in conflict management, 59–60

butobuto, *see* Modernity

C

Case method in legal anthropology, 3, 5, 6, 7, 95, 109, 147

Causation, Aristotelian, 35, 36–37fn2

Causation, communicative, 21–22, 27, 111–113, 123–124

Causation, primary, 22, 34

Causation, physical, 22, 34–35, 112–113

Causation, regimes of, 34, 37 (fig. 2.1, 2.2)

Chiefs, *see* turaga

Chiefly language, 10–11

Chiefly succession, 49, 55–56

Chiefly tradition as control discourse, 130ff

Church organization, 77fn2, 136

Civil rights struggle in U.S., viewed by Fijians, 14–15

Clowning, 45, 73

Cobo, ceremonial clapping, 42

Communication, role in conflict management, 25–26

Communication system, xv, xvi, xviii, 21, 37–38, 47, 72–73, 111–112, 123–124

Communicative causation, contrasted with "scientific," 29–31

Communication event and conflict management, 75, 80, 84 05

Comparative law project, 1–2

Conflict communities, 100

Control communication, 72–73, 112, 124, 131, 132–133, 140, 146

Constructionism, view of language in conflict, 21, 26, 113, 118, 119ff

Conversation analysis, xii, xiv

Coups, military in Fiji, 126ff
  as societal conflict, 133

Cross-cousin relationship, *see* Veitavaleni

D

Dance
  as exchange, 43–45
  as joking, *see* Clowning

Debate, political discourse, 54–55, 57, 71, 134

Discourse analysis, big and little traditions, xiff, 125

Discourse pluralism, 124, 130ff

Discourse, total systems of in conflict, 129–130

Southern Illinois Univ.-Carb.

The world of talk on a Fijian island : a
31611000984384
Due: 10/11/2000